COMPUTE-IT

COMPUTING
FOR KS3

MARK DORLING
AND GEORGE ROUSE
Series Editors

DYNAMIC
LEARNING

HODDER
EDUCATION
AN HACHETTE UK COMPANY

CAS recommends this product because it meets the aims of supporting the teaching of computer science within computing to Key Stage 3 pupils. This book supports good practice in teaching the computing curriculum which will help develop computational thinking. It describes good pedagogical strategies and offers progression throughout.

CAS is a grass roots organisation, whose energy, creativity, and leadership comes from its members. We are a collaborative partner with the BCS through the BCS Academy of Computing, and have formal support from other industry partners. Membership is open to everyone, and is very broad, including teachers, parents, governors, exam boards, industry, professional societies, and universities. We speak for the discipline of computing at school level (including FE), and not for any particular interest group. The CAS community has been instrumental in the development of the new curriculum and are 100% committed to supporting all teachers as they engage with computing, and in particular computer science. It contributes to the national debates and consultation regarding the curriculum, assessment, specifications and resources for teaching and learning. It has the aim of promoting and supporting excellence in computer science education.

Further teaching resources are available through the CAS community at:
http://community.computingatschool.org.uk

Hachette UK's policy is to use papers that are natural, renewable and recyclable products and made from wood grown in well-managed forests and other controlled sources. The logging and manufacturing processes are expected to conform to the environmental regulations of the country of origin.

Although every effort has been made to ensure that website addresses are correct at time of going to press, Hodder Education cannot be held responsible for the content of any website mentioned. It is sometimes possible to find a relocated web page by typing in the address of the home page for a website in the URL window of your browser.

Orders: please contact Hachette UK Distribution, Hely Hutchinson Centre, Milton Road, Didcot, Oxfordshire, OX11 7HH. Telephone: +44 (0)1235 827827. Email education@hachette.co.uk Lines are open from 9 a.m. to 5 p.m., Monday to Friday. You can also order through our website: www.hoddereducation.co.uk

© Apps for Good, Mark Clarkson, Mark Dorling, Caroline Ghali, Graham Hastings, Pete Marshman, Jason Pitt, Bob Reeves, George Rouse, Torsten Stauch, Carl Turland, Abigail Woodman Limited 2014.

First published in 2014 by

Hodder Education
An Hachette UK Company,
Carmelite House, 50 Victoria Embankment
London EC4Y 0DZ

Impression number   12
Year   2024

Cover photo © adimas – Fotolia

Typeset in ITC Veljovic Std by Phoenix Photosetting, Chatham, Kent.

Printed in Italy

A catalogue record for this title is available from the British Library.

ISBN 978 1 471 801815

Contents

Introduction

Computing drives innovation in the sciences, in engineering, business, entertainment and education. It touches every aspect of our lives, from the cars we drive to the movies we watch and the way in which businesses and governments communicate with and hear from us.

An understanding of Computer Science is essential if you want to keep up with changing technology and take advantage of the opportunities it offers in your life – whether it's as a career or a way of problem solving, or as a way of providing you with a greater appreciation of the way things work.

Computing is a relatively modern area of study but its roots go back to ancient times when our ancestors created calculating devices – long before modern-day calculators came into being. As you'll see, Computer Science also has a rich history of innovation and design.

While it is almost impossible to accurately predict what technological developments will happen next, there are underlying Computer Science concepts and principles that lead to future developments. These can be recognised and applied by people who work in computing.

Computational Thinking is one of these processes and it underpins all the learning in this Student's Book. This should provide you with an approach to problem solving that you will be able to use in relation to a wide range of computer-related and non-computer-related situations. By studying Computer Science you will develop valuable skills that will enable you to solve deep, multi-layered problems.

Throughout this Student's Book we have described the processes that led to the development of major ideas and systems. This will give you a much better understanding of how computing has come to be as it is today. We look at the development of computing through time, from ancient calculating devices to modern technology, highlighting how each breakthrough or development has contributed to modern Computer Science. We look at the elements that make much of the technology we all take for granted today actually work, and we look at how you can apply this knowledge and these skills to computing challenges.

Each unit in the Student's Book centres around a challenge and, in order to gain the knowledge and skills you require to complete each challenge, you will come across three different types of activity:

- **Think-IT**: These are thinking and discussion activities to get you thinking about ideas and concepts.
- **Plan-IT**: These are planning exercises that set the scene for the practical activities.
- **Compute-IT**: These are the practical computing or 'doing' activities that will allow you to apply the skills and knowledge that you have developed within the unit.

We hope that you enjoy the challenges we have set you and your study of computing.

Mark Dorling and George Rouse

Cracking the code: binary characters, cyphers and encryption

Challenge

Your challenge is to act as a secret agent who needs to send a classified message, via email, to a fellow-spy in another country. Eavesdroppers can read messages on the internet. Therefore, you need to encrypt messages to ensure that they can only be understood by your colleague. You will have to invent a cypher or secret code that only the two of you understand.

1.1 Binary coding systems

Binary: A quick reminder

All computers process data in digital form. This means that the processor inside a computer works by manipulating zeros and ones, known as binary code. The term **data representation** refers to the way that binary codes are used to represent different types of data. You already know, from *Compute-IT 1 Unit 2* and *Compute-IT 2 Unit 3*, how numbers can be represented using binary codes.

Key term

Data representation: The way that binary codes are used to represent different types of data, for example numbers and letters.

Think-IT

1.1.1 Convert the following binary into decimal numbers:

a) 00000001
b) 01101100
c) 11001100
d) 10001001
e) 11111110

1.1.2 Using as few bits as possible, convert the following decimal numbers into binary:

a) 8
b) 33
c) 130
d) 200
e) 255

1.1.3 How many different numbers can you represent with 8 bits?

1.1.4 How many different numbers can you represent with 16 bits?

As well as working with numbers, computers also have to handle text, graphics, sounds and films. The computer can only deal with all these different types of information if they are in binary form. This means that there has to be a method for converting all this information into binary code, into zeros and ones, just as you converted decimal numbers into binary in 1.1.2 Think-IT.

There are a few different systems for converting text to binary and we are going to concentrate on the most common ones. All systems have been developed to convert the letters of the alphabet, as well as punctuation marks and other characters on the keyboard.

For any system to work, everyone has to agree on the rules. Morse Code is a binary system that uses dots and dashes to represent letters. Samuel Morse invented the system over 150 years ago. He decided that when transmitting messages, dot-dash would mean the letter A, dash-dot-dot-dot would mean the letter B and so on. The system works because everyone using the code sticks to the rules.

ASCII

ASCII (pronounced as-kee) stands for the American Standard Code for Information Interchange and is a system developed in the 1960s for transferring data electronically. The original version was a 7-bit code, although more modern versions use more bits. ASCII has a binary code for all of the characters in the English language as well as special characters. For example, 1000011, which you could convert to the decimal number 67, represents an upper case 'C' in the ASCII system.

Think-IT

1.1.5 **a)** How many different characters could be represented using 7 bits?

b) How many different characters are there on a standard keyboard?

c) Do you think a 7-bit code provides enough bits to represent all the characters in the English language? What about other languages?

Plan-IT

1.1.6 Here is a small extract of the ASCII chart. It shows the 7-bit codes for the (upper case) letters of the alphabet.

Decode the following message by converting the numbers into binary and then working out which letter each binary code stands for using ASCII:

83 69 78 68 72 69 76 80

1000001	A	1001110	N
1000010	B	1001111	O
1000011	C	1010000	P
1000100	D	1010001	Q
1000101	E	1010010	R
1000110	F	1010011	S
1000111	G	1010100	T
1001000	H	1010101	U
1001001	I	1010110	V
1001010	J	1010111	W
1001011	K	1011000	X
1001100	L	1011001	Y
1001101	M	1011010	Z

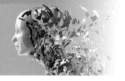
Compute-IT

1.1.7   **a)** Create a spreadsheet that will automatically convert decimal numbers into their binary equivalent and into the corresponding ASCII letter. For example, if you type in the number 71, it will show you the binary code '1000111' and the letter 'G'. Set the spreadsheet up so that it can be used to read and write short messages.

b) Extend your spreadsheet so that it can also be used to convert:
- binary codes into decimal numbers and ASCII letters, and
- ASCII letters into binary codes and decimal numbers.

Other character coding systems

There are several other systems that convert binary code into text, including Baudot, EBCDIC and Unicode.

Baudot is a 5-bit code invented in the 1870s and was used to send messages using teleprinters. These were machines designed to transmit data as a series of on and off signals down telephone wires and across radio waves. The keyboards on early teleprinters had just five keys and operators had to memorise the 5-bit codes. It was quite common for people to make mistakes when they were typing in the codes, which is why a proper keyboard, a bit like an old typewriter, was developed to make it easier to type in the messages.

▲ An operator using a teleprinter, on the left with a five-key keyboard and on the right with a typewriter keyboard

Baudot was the forerunner of all the codes that we use today, including ASCII. Although it is an old system, the expression 'baud rate' is still used today to measure how fast data can be sent.

EBCDIC – or Extended Binary Coded Decimal Interchange Code – is a code that was mainly used on large IBM mainframe computers in the1960s. At the time, these computers were not programmed by typing commands into a keyboard. Instead, the program was created using 'punched cards', with the holes in the card representing different characters and numbers. A special card reader was used to input the program into the computer. IBM invented EBCDIC as an 8-bit code for use on their own computer systems. However, as other codes became more popular IBM stopped using it and started using ASCII instead.

Unicode is a more modern code and is one of the main standards used today for converting binary into text. The codes we have looked at so far use 5, 7 or 8 bits and can therefore only represent a relatively small number of characters. Unicode uses 16 bits, which means that it can represent many more characters.

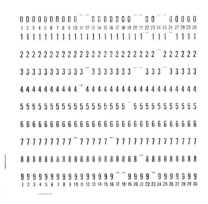

▲ A punched card used to program an IBM mainframe computer in the 1950s and 1960s

Coding system	Number of bits	Number of possible characters
Baudot	5	32
ASCII	7	128
EBCDIC	8	256
Unicode	16	65 536

▲ A table showing the number of possible characters the coding systems can represent

Think-IT

1.1.8 Find out about Unicode.

   a) When was the system invented?

   b) Why was it invented?

   c) What are the advantages of Unicode compared to ASCII?

   d) Why has Unicode become the standard way of converting binary to text?

   e) How does it work?

Think-IT

1.1.9 You have found out about Baudot, EBCDIC, ASCII and Unicode. Some of these systems are still used today and some are not. There are also other systems we have not looked at including, ISO 8859, Code Pages, ANSI and Teletext. Put all the character coding systems in chronological order. Then explain why each new system was developed and the main advantages of each system.

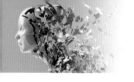
1.2 The basics of encryption

What is encryption?

Once text has been converted to binary, it is in a format that can be stored and transmitted electronically. A lot of the data stored on computers may be personal or sensitive and therefore needs to be transferred and held securely. In many cases this means that the data must be encrypted so that it cannot be understood if the wrong person gets hold of it. Encryption is the name given to the process of converting data into a secret code that can only be understood if you know the key. Decryption is the name given to the process of converting encrypted data, called cyphertext, back into its unencrypted form, called plaintext. A **cypher** is an algorithm to encrypt data so that the data can be kept secret. Data can be encrypted and decrypted using cyphers.

Why do we need encryption?

Computers are a very important part of our lives and your personal details are stored on lots of databases already. For example, your school will hold personal details about you, including your address and phone number. Your doctor will store information about your health. Social networking sites store all the information you put on your profile. As you get older, more and more of your information will be stored. For example, if you buy something online, your bank details will be used and stored for at least the duration of the purchase.

All organisations, including the government, schools, hospitals, doctors and banks, have a legal responsibility to look after all of the information they store and to keep it secure. However, there will be times when they need to send information over the internet. For example, all doctor's surgeries have an online system to book appointments with local hospitals. This means that your personal health information is being transmitted and could be snooped on or eavesdropped.

There are some situations where keeping information secure could be a matter of national security. In fact, the idea of using secret codes has been around for thousands of years, with many of them used during times of war and conflict.

The timeline on pages 8 and 9 explores key events in the history of encryption.

Key term

Cypher: An algorithm to encrypt and decrypt data.

Think-IT

1.2.1   What information might people hold on a computer that they would like to keep private?

Why is encryption so important?

Let's look at just one example to illustrate why encryption is so important: the work carried out at Bletchley Park during the Second World War.

The Enigma machine

In the early 1920s, after the end of the First World War, a German engineer called Arthur Scherbius invented the Enigma machine. It scrambled messages before sending them using telegraph wires and radio signals. Initially it was used commercially, for banking transfers, but was later adapted by the German military. The messages they sent contained classified information about their military strategies and plans for winning the war.

wheels

light bulbs

keyboard

plugs

   The messages were scrambled using a substitution cypher. In a substitution cypher each letter is 'substituted' with a different letter. For example, 'A' became 'Z' and 'B' became 'Y' and so on. The clever thing about the Enigma cypher was that each letter typed into the keyboard was substituted with a different letter every time a letter was entered, making it almost impossible to work out the code. The Enigma machine had several different wheels, each with the alphabet on them. The wheels could be turned to different positions to give different results. The machine was able to produce over 150 million, million, million possible combinations.

Breaking the code

The Enigma code was first broken by the Polish Cipher Bureau in 1932. Three Polish cryptologists – Marian Rejewski, Jerzy Rozycki and Henryk Zygalski – worked it out using mathematics and information supplied by French military intelligence. Alan Turing and his colleagues at Bletchley Park then built on their work. It wasn't until a German Enigma operator made mistakes and a book of cypher keys and an Enigma machine were captured from a German submarine that allied cryptologists were able to fully decrypt the messages.

   The cypher is the algorithm used to encrypt and decrypt a message. You might know the cypher used and how the encryption was performed but, without the key to decrypt the cyphertext, you cannot turn it into plaintext.

Think-IT

1.2.2 Although many of the cyphers on pages 8 and 9 appear quite different, many of them are based on the same underlying principles or algorithmic thinking. Research the use of cyphers through time and prepare a short presentation on their similarities.

The history of encryption

▲ An early Egyptian cypher

742 BC: The ancient Greeks invent the scytale, where messages are written on strips of paper and only make sense if the paper is wound around a stick of the correct length and diameter.

About 50 BC: Julius Caesar uses a shift cypher system, which is a type of substitution cypher, for all of his personal correspondence. It becomes known as the Caesar cypher and the basic method is still used today.

1467: The first ever substitution cypher, the Alberti Cypher, which uses two rotating disks, is invented in Italy. The same concept is used nearly 500 years later during the Second World War.

1586: Supporters of Mary Queen of Scots use coded letters in a plot to assassinate Elizabeth I. Elizabeth's spies cracked the code, leading to Mary's execution.

1605: The philosopher Francis Bacon uses steganography to create various cyphers and other ways of hiding messages within text. He invents a system for converting letters into 5-bit codes long before the binary system is developed.

1900 BC: Early cyphers are carved into monuments in ancient Egypt. It is thought they are carved for fun!

800–600 BC: Ancient Greeks use cyphers to send messages about military matters. They develop the Polybius Square as a method of sending signals using smoke or torches.

▲ An ancient Greek scytale

AD 800–900: Arabic mathematicians are the first to write down the theories of cryptography, including all the main methods for writing and cracking codes.

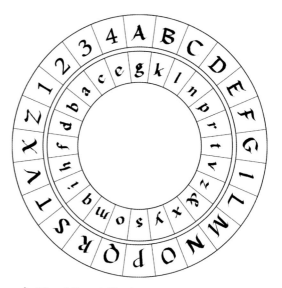

▲ The Alberti Cypher

▲ Thomas Jefferson's wooden cylinder

1797: Thomas Jefferson invents a wooden cylinder with several wheels. The letters of the alphabet are printed on each wheel and each wheel has to be in the correct position for the message to be read off the cylinder.

1789–1815: Napoleon Bonaparte develops his own cyphers to transmit sensitive military information during the French Revolution and the Napoleonic Wars.

1938–1945: Creating and breaking codes is critical to success in both world wars. In particular, the work of Alan Turing at Bletchley Park during the Second World War is viewed as one of the reasons the Allies won the war in 1945. This is because the allies were able to crack the German cyphers in order to read their secret messages.

1961: The first ever computer password is created at the Massachusetts Institute of Technology (MIT) to prevent students from wasting precious computer time!

1995: The term 'hacker' becomes a popular way of describing someone who tries to break into a computer system illegally. Originally the term was used as a name for people who were employed by computer companies to find errors and mistakes in their programs.

▲ The Enigma machine, a device used in the 20th century to encrypt and decrypt secret messages

Today: Modern cryptography is used on a very wide range of personal and public applications, from encrypting a single file on your own PC to highly complicated encryption of government secrets.

1.3 Understanding encryption and decryption

A simple cypher

Encryption is the process of taking plaintext and turning it into incomprehensible or indecipherable code, which is known as cyphertext. **Decryption** is the process of turning the cyphertext back into plaintext so that it can be understood.

The aim of encryption is to keep data secure so that if the wrong person gets hold of it, it will make no sense to them. Therefore, to decrypt the data, you need to know the 'key'. If you don't know the key you have to try to 'crack' it.

The process of encryption works like this:

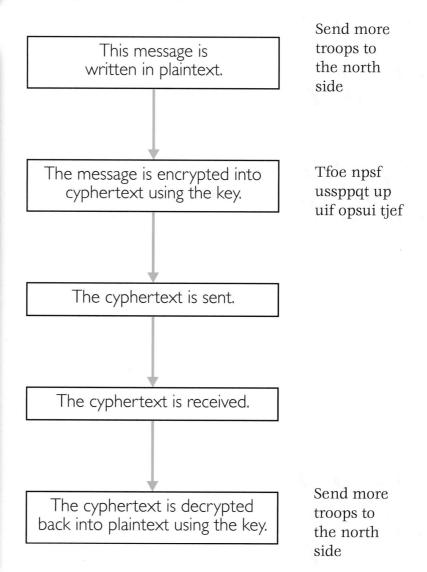

Key terms

Encryption: The process of converting data into cyphertext so that it can only be understood if you know the key.

Decryption: The process of converting encrypted data back into plaintext.

Compute-IT

1.3.1 **a)** The message below has been encrypted to keep it secure. Do you have any idea what the message says? Can you crack the code?

Uijt jt b tjnqmf dzqifs

b) This message uses the same cypher. Look at the pattern of letters. The most frequently used letters in the English language are 'e' and 't'. Does this help?

Uif difftf jt po uif ubcmf

Compute-IT

1.3.2   Here is a screenshot from a spreadsheet that can be used to crack the code used in 1.3.1 Compute-IT. How does the cypher work?

B5	▼	f_x	=VLOOKUP(B4,Sheet2!$A$1:$B$26,2)									
	A	B	C	D	E	F	G	H	I	J	K	L	M
1	Type a message into the yellow cells. Type one letter per cell.											
2	Your coded message will appear in the cells below.											
3												
4	Plain text	t	h	i	s	i	s	a	c	o	d	e
5	Cypher text	U	I	J	T	J	T	B	D	P	E	F
6												
7												
8												

Common methods for encrypting data

There are several common methods for encrypting data.

Reverse cypher

This is perhaps the simplest code to crack, because all you do is reverse the message.

'THE EAGLE HAS LANDED' becomes 'DEDNAL SAH ELGAE EHT'.

You could make it a bit harder by removing the spaces: 'DEDNALSAHELGAEEHT'.

Or by grouping the letters together in groups of the same length to disguise the words: 'DED NAL SAH ELG AEE HT'.

Substitution cypher

In a substitution cypher, each letter of the alphabet is changed – substituted – for another character. This is sometimes called a Caesar Cypher. The cypher used in 1.3.1 Compute-IT and 1.3.2 Compute-IT is a simple substitution cypher. Every letter of plaintext is substituted with the letter that is one ahead of it in the alphabet. This is sometimes called a 'shift' as every letter has shifted a set number of places.

The diagram below shows a substitution cypher with a two-letter shift. If encrypted with this cypher, the message 'THE EAGLE HAS LANDED' becomes 'VJG GCING JCU NCOFGF'.

Plan-IT

1.3.3   **a)** Write a message using a reverse cypher. Make it as difficult as possible to crack.

   b) Pass your cyphertext to someone else and see if they can crack it.

A	B	C	D	E	F	G	H	I	J	K	L	M	N	O	P	Q	R	S	T	U	V	W	X	Y	Z
C	D	E	F	G	H	I	J	K	L	M	N	O	P	Q	R	S	T	U	V	W	X	Y	Z	A	B

There are different ways of creating substitution cyphers to make them harder to decrypt. One method is to use a keyword. For example, you might select the word 'chopstick'.

First, you delete any repeated letters in your keyword. 'Chopstick' becomes 'chopstik'.

Next you substitute the first eight letters of the alphabet with the letters from your keyword.

Then you add the remaining letters in alphabetical order.

If encrypted with this cypher, 'THE EAGLE HAS LANDED' becomes 'RKS SCIES KCE ECGPSP'.

Plan-IT

1.3.4 a) Create your own substitution cypher and write a message using it.

b) Pass your message to someone else and see if they can crack it. Then give them the key to your cypher and see if they are able to decrypt it.

Another variation on a substitution cypher is to substitute letters for symbols. This is what the Pigpen Cypher does. Different letters of the alphabet are placed into different grids. The section of the grid that contains each letter has a unique shape, which becomes a symbol in the code.

The Pigpen alphabet therefore looks like this:

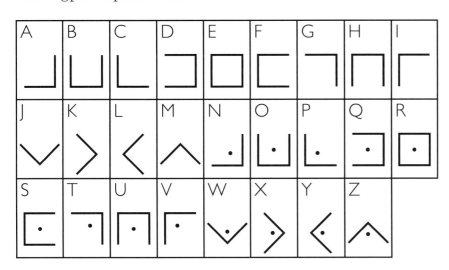

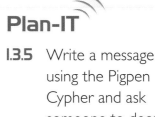

Plan-IT

1.3.5   Write a message using the Pigpen Cypher and ask someone to decode it. Or develop your own substitution cypher that does not use letters.

Modulo 2 encoding

During the Second World War, a German engineering company called Lorenz developed a system for sending secret messages. In simple terms, the code used a method called Modulo 2 addition, which was a way of creating a substitution cypher.

Every letter is given a 5-bit binary code. Then the binary codes are added together using Modulo 2 addition, to create a new binary code, which in turn represents a new letter. The key is added to the plaintext to create the cyphertext.

The lookup table Lorenz used is as shown here.

For example, if we choose 'A' or 11000 as our key we can encrypt the letter 'B' by adding 'A' to 'B':

$$
\begin{array}{r}
1\,1\,0\,0\,0 \\
+\quad\ \\
1\,0\,0\,1\,1 \\
\hline
0\,1\,0\,1\,1
\end{array}
$$

A	11000	N	00110
B	10011	O	00011
C	01110	P	01101
D	10010	Q	11101
E	10000	R	01010
F	10110	S	10100
G	01011	T	00001
H	00101	U	11100
I	01100	V	01111
J	11010	W	11101
K	11110	X	10111
L	01001	Y	10101
M	00111	Z	10001

Plan-IT

I.3.6 **a)** Using the same table that Lorenz used, encrypt a message using the Modulo 2 addition method.

b) Pass your code and the key to someone else and see if they can decrypt your message.

This could also be shown as an (A OR B) truth table with the two letters shown as the inputs, and the encrypted letter shown as the output.

Input		Output
A	**B**	
I	I	0
I	0	I
0	0	0
0	I	I
0	I	I

Looking at the lookup table on page 13 we can see that 01011 is the code for the letter 'G'. A + B = G. Therefore, when it is encrypted, 'B' becomes 'G'.

Transposition cyphers

With transposition cyphers, the letters of the message are rearranged – transposed – to form an anagram. The letters must be rearranged according to a set pattern or it will be much more difficult to decrypt the message. One way of doing this is called the railfence method, where the message is split across several lines. For example:

T	E	A	L	H	S	A	D	D
H	E	G	E	A	L	N	E	

becomes, if you read it line by line: 'TEALHSADDHEGEALNE'.

If you were decrypting this message you would need to know that the key is that it has been split over two lines.

You can use any number of lines. For example, you could put the message across three lines:

T			A		H		A		D
	H	E	G	E	A	L	N	E	
	E		L		S		D		

In this case, the message becomes: 'TAHADHEGEALNEELSD'.

With the route method the letters are placed into a grid, working from top to bottom, filling the first column before moving on to the second. For example, 'THE EAGLE HAS LANDED' can be placed into a 6 × 3 grid as follows:

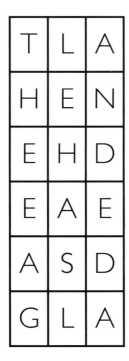

becoming 'TLAHENEHDEAEASDGLA'. Notice that you can add 'null' or meaningless values if you have spare cells in your grid. In this case, the letter A has been added to the bottom right-hand cell.

If you were decrypting this message you would need to know the dimensions of the grid.

Plan-IT

1.3.7 **a)** Using first the railfence method and then the route method, encrypt a message using a transposition cypher.

b) Pass your code and the key to someone else and see if they can decrypt your message.

1.4 Using a spreadsheet to encrypt and decrypt data

▲ An old fashioned cypher machine

It is possible to program a cypher using the functions available with spreadsheet software.

Functions for binary coding

There are two functions in spreadsheet software that are particularly useful when handling binary codes. The first is DEC2BIN, which converts decimals into binary, and the second is BIN2DEC, which converts binary to decimal.

Both these functions work in a similar way to the spreadsheet you created for 1.1.7 Compute-IT. However, rather than place the lookup table on a separate worksheet, the spreadsheet application stores it internally.

Another useful function is CHAR, which converts a number into an ASCII character. The number must be between 0 and 255 as these are the only numbers used by the 7-bit ASCII code.

B3	▼	fx	=DEC2BIN(B2)	
	A	B	C	D
1				
2	Decimal	176		
3	Binary	10110000		
4				

◀ DEC2BIN in **Excel**

B3	▼	fx	=BIN2DEC(B2)	
	A	B	C	D
1				
2	Binary	1001001		
3	Decimal	73		
4				

◀ BIN2DEC in **Excel**

B3	▼	fx	=CHAR(B2)
	A	B	C
1			
2	Decimal	65	
3	ASCII character	A	
4			

◀ CHAR in **Excel**

Functions for conditional statements

VLOOKUP is a conditional statement. The lookup table looks at the value typed into a cell and, if it meets a specific condition in another cell or a range of cells, it performs a set action. For example, in the spreadsheet on the next page.

1 A letter is typed into cell A4.
2 The value in the cell is compared to the lookup table contained within the cell range A1 to B26 on Sheet 2.

Notice that absolute referencing is used and is shown by the $ sign. If the $ sign is placed before part of the spreadsheet cell reference that part of the reference is not changed when the cell contents are copied. In this case, when the formula `VLOOKUP(A4,Sheet2!$A$1:$B$26,2)` is copied across the sheet the value A4 changes to B4, C4 etc. but the reference to the table on Sheet 2, `$A$1:$B$26,2` does not change. This means the formula can be copied and pasted without needing to change the cell references.

3 If the value typed in cell A4 is the same as a value in the lookup table then the condition is met and the value in the second column of the lookup table is placed in the cell that contains the formula.

4 If the value is not contained in the lookup table then the condition is not met and `#N/A` or 'Not applicable' is placed in the cell that contains the formula.

A5		f_x	=VLOOKUP(A4,Sheet2!$A$1:$B$26,2)								
	A	B	C	D	E	F	G	H	I	J	K
1	Type a message into the yellow cells. Type one letter per cell.										
2	Your coded message will appear in the cells below.										
3											
4	t	h	i	s	i	s	a	c	o	d	e
5	U	I	J	T	J	T	B	D	P	E	F
6											

As you know, 'if' statements are also conditional statements. IF the condition is met – is true – then one course of action is taken, but IF the condition is not met – is false – then another course of action is taken.

The spreadsheet below has been set up to help a code breaker decide which disk to use to create an Alberti Cypher. There are two disks, Disk A and Disk B. The RANDBETWEEN function is used to generate a random number between 0 and 500. If the number is 250 or less, then Disk A is used. If the number is greater than 250, then Disk B is used.

B4		f_x	=IF(B3<250,"A","B")	
	A		B	C
1	Spreadsheet to select a disk for an Alberti Cypher			
2				
3	Press F9 to generate a random number		166	
4	Disk to use		A	
5				

The format of the 'if' statement is
`=IF(condition, what to do if true, what to do if false)`
   You can also nest 'if' statements to cover a wider range of conditions. For example, if there were five disks to choose from, you could set up a nested 'if' statement as follows:

Think-IT

1.4.1   Describe, in natural language, the nested 'if' statements in the screenshot below.

| B4 | ▼ | f_x | =IF(B3<100,"A",IF(B3<200,"B",IF(B3<300,"C",IF(B3<400,"D","E")))) |

	A	B	C	D	E	F
1	**Spreadsheet to select a disk for an Alberti Cypher**					
2						
3	Press F9 to generate a random number	11				
4	Disk to use	A				
5						
6						

Functions for modulo 2

MOD calculates the remainder when a number is divided by the modulo value. For example MOD(11,3) would be 2, because 3 divides into 11 three times with a remainder of 2. If you set the modulo value to 2, the MOD(X,2) function will return either '0' or '1', the only possible remainders when dividing by 2.

| D4 | ▼ | f_x | =MOD(B4+C4,2) |

	A	B	C	D	E
1	**Using the MOD function to create a truth table**				
2					
3		A	B	Output	
4		1	1	0	
5		1	0	1	
6		0	0	0	
7		0	1	1	
8		0	1	1	
9					

▲ This spreadsheet shows how MOD can be used to create an (A OR B) truth table.

Compute-IT

1.4.2   Using spreadsheet software, write programs to encrypt and decrypt data. You can use any of the cyphers that you have learned about in this unit.

1.5 Using a programming language to encrypt data

It is possible to program a cypher using a suitable programming language. Most programming languages support similar features to the spreadsheet features we have seen already, but the examples used are coded in Python version 3.

Working with strings and built-in functions

A string is a list of characters, so you work with strings to manipulate characters to create cyphertext. To join two strings together we **concatenate** them by combining them one after the other.

```
plainText1 = input('Enter your name: ')
plainText2 = 'Hello '
plaintext = plainText2 + plainText1
print(plainText3)
```

Working with functions

Built-in **functions** are procedures that are very common and so are already defined within the programming language. For example, the `print` and `input` functions are needed in so many programs that they are already set up ready for the programmer to use.

User-defined functions can be created for any procedure or block of code. If you are writing a program and there is a procedure that you know you will need to use again, you can put this into a function. You can then just call the function when you need it in your program rather than having to repeat the code every time. Decomposing your program into functions makes it simpler, removes duplication and means the program is less likely to contain errors.

Functions require information to make them work. For example, if you were using the 'print' function, you need to tell the program what to print. `print(cypherText)` tells the program to print the current value of the variable called 'cypherText'. The information needed to make a function work is called a **parameter**. When we call a function we pass it the parameter we want it to use.

> **Key term**
>
> **Concatenate**: To join two strings of characters together to create a single string.

> **plainText2 and plainText1 are concatenated to produce the output plainText3.**

> **Key term**
>
> **Function**: A subprogram that carries out a specific task. Some functions are 'built-in' to a programming language. Programmers can also create their own 'user-defined' functions.

> **Key term**
>
> **Parameter**: The information supplied to a function.

The 'def' keyword is used to create a function called `shiftCypher`.

This is the parameter that will be passed into the function. It is a variable called `plainText`.

```
def shiftCypher(plainText)
```

This is where the subprogram that creates the cyphertext is typed.

```
return cypherText
```

Once the code that creates the cyphertext has run the function returns a value, called `cypherText`, to the main program.

The parameter `plainText`, which is passed to the function in the example above, is a **local variable**. It can only be used within the function. If the function is called again we pass it a new parameter and the function will use the new value.

String length and indexing

You may need to select individual characters from a string. For example, a reverse cypher requires you to select the last character in the plaintext and make it the first character in the cyphertext.

> **Key term**
>
> **Local variable**: A variable that can only be used inside a function and not anywhere else within the program. A global variable can be used anywhere in a program and its functions.

1	2	3	4	5	6	7	8	9	10	11	12	13	14	15	16	17
T	H	E	E	A	G	L	E	H	A	S	L	A	N	D	E	D

Here we need to select the character in position 17 and put it in position 1, then select the character in position 16 and put it in position 2 and so on. To do this, we first need to work out the length of the string:

```
plainText = input('Enter message: ')
n = len(plainText)
print(n)
```

`len` is a built-in function that calculates the length of the string.

A value, equal to the number of characters in the `plaintext` input, is printed.

Strings of characters can be considered lists and each individual character can be identified by its place in the list, or index. For example, if the user types in, 'The eagle has landed', the string is 20 characters in length including the spaces. `plainText[0]` would be 'T', `plainText[1]` would be 'h' and so on.

Conditional statements

Here is an example of a 'while' statement in Python version 3:

```
while password == correct
    print("Correct password")
    # allow access to computer
# deny access to computer
print("Access denied")
```

While the condition is true, the program performs the action in the indented block of code. If the condition is false, the program performs a different action. In this example, if the password is correct access to the computer is allowed, but if it is incorrect then access is denied.

Another type of conditional statement is the 'if else' statement:

This program checks the grade that is entered and then prints a message to the screen stating that the grade is a distinction, a merit, a pass or a fail. Notice Python provides an `elif` clause within an `if` statement. This is short for 'else if', and removes the need for multiple 'if else' statements.

```
testScore = input('Enter Grade')
if testScore == 'A':
    print('Well done, you got a distinction')
elif testScore == 'B':
    print('Well done, you got a merit')
elif testScore == 'C':
    print('Well done, you passed')
else:
    print('Sorry, you failed this time')
```

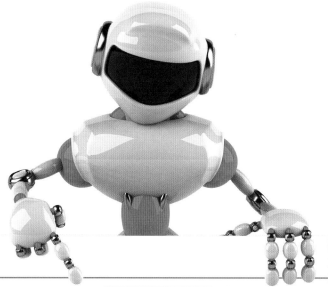

Challenge

Do you remember the challenge for this unit, to act as a secret agent who needs to send a classified message, via email, to a fellow-spy in another country? Eavesdroppers can read messages on the internet. Therefore, you need to encrypt messages to ensure that they can only be understood by your colleague. You will have to invent a cypher or secret code that only the two of you understand.

Compute-IT

1.5.1   Write a program that will keep your messages secure by encrypting and decrypting data using a suitable cypher. Select the most appropriate cypher for the task and code it in a suitable text-based programming language. Justify your choice of cypher.

Unit 2 Representing sounds

Challenge

A local record label wants to open its own independent music store that allows users to stream music live to their mobile digital devices over 3G. They need you to help devise a compression strategy that will allow them to keep the file size down without compromising on sound quality.

2.1 File sizes and bandwidth

Measuring file size

All computer files are stored as a series of 1s and 0s. Numbers, letters, pictures, videos and sounds are all stored in the same way and it is important to understand how we measure file size so we know how big files are likely to be, especially if we intend to stream them to mobile digital devices over a 3G network.

Think-IT

2.1.1 Based on your experience of media files, put the following types of files into size order.

A A DVD film

B A tiny text file, which can be defined as a file of 10,000 characters or 150 lines

C A BluRay film

D A 6-page Word document

E A 4-minute song saved as an MP3

Internet connection speeds are measured in bits per second. So, for example, we need to be able to work out how many bits there are in a 6 MB MP3 file.

Think-IT

2.1.2 Calculate how many bits there are in the following files:

a) 130 KB

b) 8 MB

c) 5 GB

bit

byte (8 bits)

kilobyte (1024 bytes)

megabyte (1024 KB)

gigabyte (1024 MB)

terabyte (1024 GB)

6 megabytes	= 6 × 1024 kilobytes	= 6144 kilobytes
6144 kilobytes	= 6144 × 1024 bytes	= 6 291 456 bytes
6 291 456 bytes	= 6 291 456 × 8 bits	= 50 331 648 bits

▲ Calculating file sizes

Measuring bandwidth

In order to work out how long it will take to send a file to a mobile digital device over a 3G network we need to know about bandwidth. **Bandwidth** is a measure of how quickly data can be downloaded or uploaded. It is usually measured in bits per second (bps) or megabits per second (mbps).

We generally refer to storage in bytes and transmission rates in bits. A capital 'B' in a file size denotes bytes, whereas a lower case 'b' refers to bits (1 byte = 8 bits). A 2 MB file is two megabytes in size, whereas a download speed of 2 mbps is two megabits (0.25 megabytes) per second.

Key term

Bandwidth: A measure of how quickly data can be downloaded or uploaded. It is usually measured in bits per second (bps) or megabits per second (mbps).

Mobile data speeds

Mobile providers usually advertise the maximum download speed for customers but the average speed is often slower. Mobile data speeds vary depending on how good the connection is and how many people in the area are using a data connection at the same time. Mobile digital devices often switch between connection types – between 3G and 2G, for example – to get the best connection speed.

Think-IT

2.1.3   Copy the table below and then carry out an internet search to complete it.

Connection type	Symbol used to indicate connection type on mobile digital device	Typical bandwidth
3G / HSPA		
Edge (2.5G)		
GPRS (2G)		

Think-IT

2.1.4   Calculate how long it will take to download a 6MB MP3 file using each connection type:

a) 3G

b) Edge

c) GPRS

Think-IT

2.1.5   Why might it be impractical for people in some areas to stream music on their mobile digital devices? Are there any reasons other than speed that might cause problems if people stream a lot of music?

What does a digital sound look like?

It might seem like a strange question, but examining what a sound *looks* like – the **waveform** of a sound – can give a valuable clue about the way sounds are stored on a computer system.

Key term

Waveform: A graphical display of a sound file.

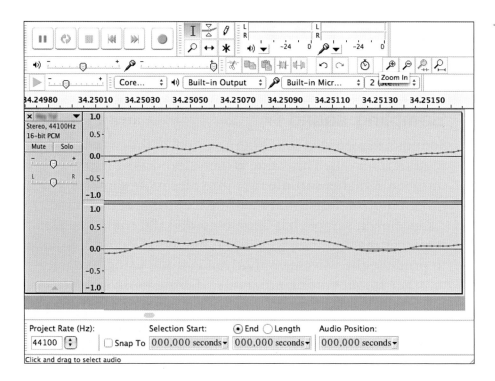

There are many programs available for recording and editing sounds. Audacity is a very good program that is completely free and works on Windows, Mac and Linux computer systems. Sound can be recorded using the large, red 'Record' button at the top of the Audacity window or existing sound files can be opened and examined. This shows a music file opened in Audacity.

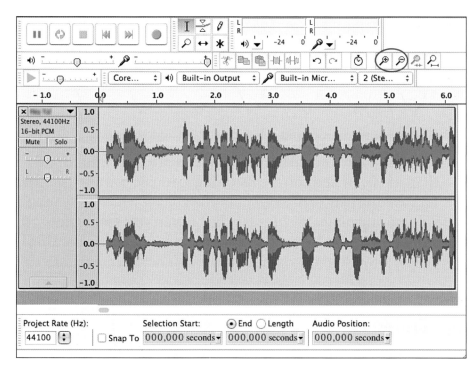

By using the 'Zoom In' icon on the right of the toolbar it is possible to take a close look at a sound file in Audacity.

Compute-IT

2.1.6   Record a sound or open an existing sound in a sound-editing program. By listening and zooming in and out, try to work out how the waveform changes depending on the volume and the pitch of the sound.

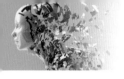

2.2 Sampling and recording sound

Sampling sound

Sounds are recorded by taking a sample of the sound at regular intervals. This value is then stored as a binary number. A higher **sample rate** provides more samples which gives a more detailed and accurate recording of the sound.

Once each sample has been recorded the computer plots it on a graph and then fills in the line between each sample to produce the waveform that you can see using Audacity or other sound-editing programs. Having more samples, or more points on the graph, makes it much easier to fill in those lines accurately.

When a sound is played, the computer sends each signal to a speaker to recreate the sound. A sound file with more samples will be more accurate than a sound file with fewer samples.

Of course more samples means that more bits are needed to store the data, so more samples means a bigger file size.

▲ This waveform is played in less than 0.001 of a second.

It is possible to record human speech at a lower sample rate than music. When you are listening to music you are listening for the interplay of instruments and voices, which vary in volume and pitch. In contrast, the human voice is a much simpler sound to listen to and so the quality of the recording can be lower without damaging the listener's enjoyment.

Think-IT

2.2.1 Go to **www. hoddereducation.co.uk/ compute-it**

Try to identify the song by listening to the three different versions.

▲ A waveform showing a piece of classical music

▲ A waveform showing a human voice

Think-IT

2.2.2 A sample rate of 1 kHz means 1000 samples per second. Calculate how many samples would be needed to store:

a) one minute of audio at 10 kHz

b) one minute of audio at 44 kHz.

2.2.3 Why might music **streamed** on a mobile digital device be of poorer quality than music **downloaded** on a mobile digital device? What decisions might the mobile network provider have taken that lead to this reduction in quality?

Most music CDs are recorded at either 44.1 kHz or at 48 kHz. At these high sample rates the recorded sound is almost indistinguishable from the original. Most landline and mobile telephone and walkie-talkie systems use a sample rate of 8 kHz. This uses only one-sixth of the samples and yet still produces a sound quality that is fine for human speech.

Sound-editing programs, such as Audacity, allow you to change the sample rate at which sound is recorded, letting you control the file size of the final sound file. Changing the sample rate of an *existing* recording is likely to speed it up or slow it down using the same number of samples and so won't change the file size.

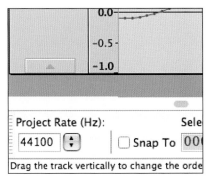

▲ The sample rate can be adjusted in Audacity. This is best done before recording starts.

Compute-IT

2.2.4 Using a sound-editing program, record sound at different sample rates and compare their quality and file size.

So far we have only thought about sound files that use one channel. Most CD and MP3 players use a two-channel system called stereo, which has a left channel and a right channel. This requires twice as much data. Many people now have surround sound systems in their homes, which use more than two channels, and they need even more data again.

Think-IT

2.2.5 What sample rate would you use in each of the following situations and why?

a) To record an album in a music-recording studio

b) To record an interview to be sent to a colleague over a poor connection

c) To record a song on a mobile phone at a concert to email to a friend

Think-IT

2.2.6 a) Copy and complete the following table to help you think about the file size requirements for different types of audio:

	Number of channels	File size for a 1-minute recording
Mono	1	720 kB
Stereo		
5.1 surround sound		
7.1 surround sound		

b) Explain how modern developments, such as the introduction of DVDs and BluRay discs have made it easier to include high-quality audio on movies and TV boxed sets.

2.3 Compressing sound files

Lossy compression

Each sample in a sound file is stored as a number, usually using either 16 or 32 bits (2 or 4 bytes). 192,000 bytes are needed for each second of music if 16 bits are used at a sample rate of 96,000 kHz. In this instance, a one-minute song would have a file size of around 11 MB. If the song was in stereo, and so needed a left channel and a right channel, it would be twice the size: 22 MB. WAV files store **uncompressed** sound files in this form. They are clearly too big for everyday use. In fact, if CDs held files of this size, albums would be no more than 32 minutes long!

If a sound file can be made smaller then it can be downloaded more quickly and more songs will fit onto a CD or onto a mobile digital device. The most common way to compress a sound file is to use the MP3 file format. MP3 uses **lossy compression** to reduce the file size.

> ### Key terms
>
> **Uncompressed**: A digital file that is stored without any attempt to make it smaller.
>
> **Lossy compression**: A method of reducing the size of a file in a way that reduces the quality of the file's contents.

Think-IT

2.3.1 Choose a paragraph with at least four or five sentences from a book and compress the meaning into a 140-character tweet. How did you do this and was the meaning still clear?

By using a variety of complex strategies an MP3 encoder can significantly reduce the size of a file. Some of these strategies involve removing parts of the sound, usually parts that are very difficult to hear.

Rather than simply changing the sample rate, the amount of compression is described using the number of bits per second needed to store the file. The bitrates typically used are 128 kbps, 160 kbps, 192 kbps and 320 kbps.

The more heavily compressed an MP3 file is, the smaller the file size and the poorer the quality of the sound. An MP3 file with the same sound quality as a track on a CD would need to be encoded at 320 kbps, which would result in a four-minute song with a file size of 9 MB. The same song encoded at 128 kbps would take up less than 4 MB but the sound quality would be slightly (though noticeably) worse. It is very rare for music files to be compressed below 128 kbps because of the loss of sound quality, although 64 kbps MP3 files are often used for speech, such as audiobooks.

Name example.wav
Kind Waveform audio
Size 23.2 MB
Created Today 11:31
Modified Today 11.31
Last opened Today 11:31
Duration 01:00
Sample rate 96,000
Bits per sample 16

▲ An uncompressed WAV file that is one minute long

▲ This is the same track saved as a high-quality MP3. The file size for a high-quality MP3 is much smaller than for a WAV file.

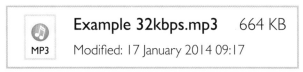

▲ An MP3 file with a very low bitrate will be very small, but will not sound very good.

Compute-IT

2.3.2 Use sound-editing software to convert a WAV file to MP3 using different bitrates and listen to the differences in sound quality.

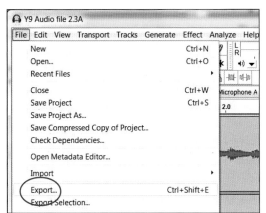

▲ To do this in Audacity, click on 'File' and select 'Export…'.

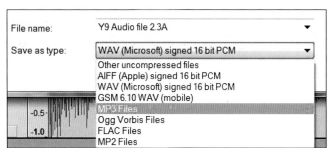

▲ Choose 'MP3 Files' from the dropdown list. Click 'Save'.

Lossless compression

Lossless compression reduces the file size of a sound file without reducing the sound quality.

The algorithms used to create a zip file are the most commonly used forms of lossless compression. While this is not often used for sound files, it is a good way to reduce the size of one file or a number of files. A zip file ends in '.zip' and is smaller than the original file. Some files shrink more than others when they are compressed as zip files, but they never lose quality. The downside of lossless compression is that the file size is not reduced by as much as it is with lossy compression.

> **Key term**
>
> **Lossless compression**: A method of reducing the size of a file in a way that does not reduce the quality of the file's contents.

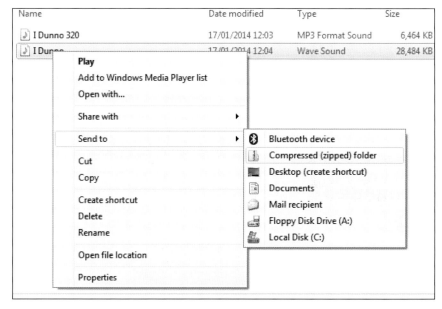

▲ To create a zip file in Windows 7, right click on a file and choose 'Send to' and 'Compressed (zipped) folder'.

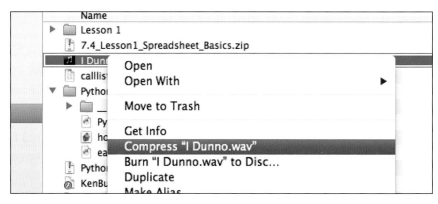

▲ To create a zip file in Mac OSX, right click on a file and choose 'Compress "filename"'.

Compute-IT

2.3.3 Compress a sound file using lossless compression by creating a zip file and then compare the file size and sound quality of files that have been compressed using lossy and lossless compression techniques. You will of course need to unzip the zip file to list to the file compressed using lossless compression.

Think-IT

2.3.4 Some people prefer to listen to lossless music using the FLAC format which is smaller than a WAV file but larger than an MP3. Why do you think some people prefer FLAC files to MP3s? Why do you think MP3 files are more commonly used?

Challenge

Do you remember the challenge for this unit? A local record label wants to open its own independent music store that allows users to stream live to their mobile digital devices over 3G and they need you to help devise a compression strategy that will allow them to keep the file size down without compromising on sound quality. You should now know everything you need to know in order to help them make an informed decision.

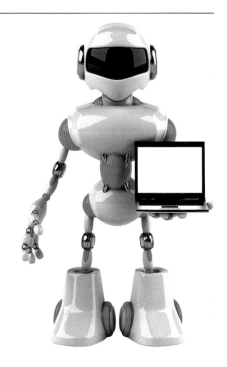

Compute-IT

2.3.5 Create a podcast that explains to the music company how they should prepare their music files ready for streaming. Your script must include information on:

- typical download speeds for mobile digital devices
- typical files sizes of WAV and MP3 files
- how the choice of sample rate will affect the file size and quality
- whether to use lossy or lossless compression, and what the downside of each choice would be.

You could also refer to the sound files you have already created.

Challenge

Nobody knows the subject of Variation XIII of Edward Elgar's *Enigma Variations*, although there are clues. Your challenge is to discover who this piece of music is about by following the clues and constructing and interrogating a database.

Think-IT

3.1.1 What data about you is stored? Where is it stored? Why?

Key terms

Database: An organised collection of data.

Field: A single item of data.

Record: A collection of related fields.

Table: A set of data elements that are organised in rows and columns. A table contains a specified number of columns but as many rows as you need.

Key field: A key field uniquely identifies each record in the database. It is known as a primary key when it is a single key field, or a composite key when a combination of fields is used.

3.1 Introduction to databases

When does data become information?

In order to make sense of data you need a context. For example, if you are given the following data:

Portland Rd, Bessie, 6

you will not be able to understand it until you are told that:

- Portland Rd is the name of a race horse, Bessie is the name of its trainer and it is six years old
- or Portland Rd is the name of a band, their album is called Bessie and it costs £6
- or you have an appointment to meet Bessie on Portland Rd at 6pm.

Once you know what the individual pieces of data mean you can start to store them together and organise them. Once your data is organised, you have a **database** from which you can extract information.

Each individual item of data in a database is called a **field**. Where a set of fields relates to a single entity, to one person or item, they are collectively known as a **record**. If you imagine a database as a **table**, the fields are the columns and the records are the rows. When one of the fields in the record uniquely identifies the record, this is called a primary key or a **key field**.

For example, you will have a student identification number so that teachers in your school know they are dealing with your information and they are not confusing you with someone else with the same name.

Think-IT

3.1.2   Think about a database that stores information about you, such as your school information system or your local library or sports club membership database. What fields do you think it contains? Which of these fields would be the key field?

Who was Edward Elgar?

▲ Edward Elgar, 1857–1934

Edward Elgar was an English composer. His pieces are often played at concerts. He wrote the *Pomp and Circumstances Marches* including *Land of Hope and Glory*, which is traditionally sung at the last night of the Proms in the Albert Hall in London. Another of his famous works is *Enigma Variations*. Each of the variations is about one of Elgar's friends.

We know the subject of all but one of the variations:

Variation **I**: C.A.E. (Caroline Alice Elgar, Elgar's wife)

Variation **II**: H.D.S.-P. (Hew Steuart-Powell, a pianist friend who often accompanied Elgar)

Variation **III**: R.B.T. (Richard Townshend, an amateur actor and mimic)

Variation **IV**: W.M.B. (William Meath Baker, a bluff, hospitable countryman)

Variation **V**: R.P.A. (Richard Arnold, son of a poet and a gifted amateur pianist)

Variation **VI**: Ysobel (Miss Ysobel Fitton, Elgar's viola pupil)

Variation **VII**: Troyte (Arthur Troyte Griffiths, who was not very good at playing the piano)

Variation **VIII**: W.N. (Winifred Norbury)

Variation **IX**: Nimrod (Augustus Jaegar, a keen huntsman and Elgar's best friend. This is the most famous variation)

Variation **X**: Dorabella (Miss Dora Penny, who had a slight hesitancy in her speech)

Variation **XI**: G.R.S. (George Sinclair, the organist of Hereford Cathedral)

Variation **XII**: B.G.N. (Basil Nevinson, an eminent cellist)

Variation **XIII**: *** (includes the clarinet quotation from Mendelssohn's *Calm Sea and Prosperous Voyage*)

Variation **XIV**: E.D.U. (Edu was Elgar's nickname. This variation is a self-portrait).

Your first clue is:
The person you are
looking for is female.

The investigation begins ...

On the next few pages are biographical descriptions of 16 of Elgar's friends and family. He could have dedicated Variation XIII to any of them.

Plan-IT

3.1.3 You are going to create a database of information about Elgar's friends. The first step in creating a database is sifting the information you have and deciding what should and should not be included in our database. The process of extracting relevant information is a form of computational thinking. It includes both analysis and abstraction when selecting the information you will need to help you solve the problem you have identified.

a) Read the biographical descriptions and identify the main facts about each person.

b) Look at your notes and pick out the information that is common to all Elgar's friends, such as their names. Then look at the information that is not common to all his friends and decide whether or not it should become part of your database.

Caroline Alice Elgar

Caroline Alice Roberts was born on 9 October 1848, in Bhooj, Gujarat, India, where her father was in the British Army. She was more commonly known by her middle name Alice. Alice was a writer and known for her poetry and novels. She also played a number of instruments and Elgar was her teacher. They fell in love and in 1889 they married. They had one daughter called Carice Irene, who was born in 1890. Alice would have travelled to and from India by ship.

Helen Weaver

In his early twenties Elgar fell in love with a musician called Helen Weaver. Helen was born on or around 15 December 1861 and was four years younger than Elgar. Her father was a shoe merchant and the family lived close to Elgar. Elgar adored her and when she went to Leipzig to study music, he followed her for a three-week holiday. Both Helen and Elgar would have travelled to Germany by ship. On her return in 1883 Elgar asked her to marry him. She agreed, but less than 18 months later broke off the engagement. All sorts of reasons have been offered for this; the fact that her parents did not agree, that she had poor health (she had tuberculosis), the death of her mother, and Elgar's uncompromising nature. Nobody really knows what happened. Elgar, however, was devastated and never fully recovered from the rejection. Helen emigrated to New Zealand, travelling by sea, and Elgar never saw her again. She led a happy life in New Zealand. Her health improved and she married a bank manager. They had two children. Helen died from cancer in 1927, aged 66.

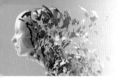

Lady Mary Lygon

Lady Mary Lygon (pronounced Liggon) was an English noblewoman. She was born on 26 February 1869 in Worcestershire. Her parents were Lord and Lady Beauchamp and she was the eldest of their five children. Lady Mary was particularly close to her brother, William, who became a politician like his father. Lady Mary was a close friend of Elgar and admired his work, often promoting him to friends. In 1899, when the *Enigma Variations* were being finished, it is rumoured that Elgar wrote to Lady Mary Lygon to ask permission to use her initials in the title of Variation XIII, but as she and her brother were on the point of setting sail for Australia (he had been appointed Governor of New South Wales) there was no time for her to send a reply and so Elgar used '***' instead. In 1905, Lady Mary married Lieutenant-Colonel Henry Hepburn-Stuart-Forbes-Trefusis and became Lady Trefusis. She died on 12 September 1927.

Beatrice Harrison

Beatrice Harrison was a British cellist who was born in Roorkee, India, on 9 December 1892 and died in 1965. She was very highly regarded and was often the first person to play pieces by composers like Delius and Elgar. The Harrison family moved back to England during Beatrice's childhood, where she studied at the Royal College of Music, London. Afterwards she studied at the High School of Music in Berlin. In 1910 she won the Mendelssohn Prize, a scholarship for promising young musicians, and made her debut in the Bechstein Hall, Berlin. Elgar and Henry Wood, an English conductor, held Beatrice in very high regard. Harrison gave the first festival performance of Edward Elgar's *Cello Concerto* outside London, at the Three Choirs Festival in Hereford in 1921. Notably, she was the soloist chosen to make the 'official' HMV recording of the concerto, with Elgar conducting, for the gramophone.

Billy Reed

William Henry 'Billy' Reed was a long-time personal friend of Edward Elgar. He was a violinist, teacher, composer and conductor. He also wrote a biography of Elgar. Born in Frome, Somerset on 29 July 1876, he was the son of an Inland Revenue Officer. From the start of the 20th century, Elgar and Billy Reed's paths crossed many times but they didn't become friends until 1910. Billy often helped Elgar out with his compositions when he was writing his violin concertos. Billy Reed was leader of the London Symphony Orchestra for 23 years, from 1912 to 1935. When Elgar's wife died in 1920, Billy Reed was part of the quartet that played a movement from Elgar's *String Quartet* at her funeral at St Wulstan's Church, Little Malvern. In 1939 he was awarded a Doctorate of Music by the University of Cambridge. He died suddenly, in Dumfries, on 2 July 1942, aged 65.

Frederick Delius

Frederick Theodore Albert Delius was an English composer. He was born on 29 January 1862 in Bradford, to a family of wealthy merchants. Delius learnt to play the piano and violin as a boy. To prepare him to join the family business, Frederick was sent to America in 1884 to manage an orange plantation. He was not interested in the work and instead started composing music, influenced by African–American music. On his return to England, he managed to convince his father to send him to the Leipzig Conservatorium to study. He moved from there to Paris, where he lived for nearly a decade. He wrote *A Village Romeo and Juliet*, which is considered a masterpiece, towards the end of the First World War. In his later years, he wrote *Caprice and Elegy* for cello and orchestra for the cellist Beatrice Harrison. A year before he died, Elgar met Delius in Leipzig and they got on very well, although Delius was not a great fan of Elgar's work! Delius married a German painter in 1903. He died at their home in Grez on 10 June 1934.

Carice Elgar

Elgar's daughter, Carice Irene Elgar, was born on 14 August 1890. Edward and Alice Elgar had no other children. The name 'Carice' is a combination of Caroline and Alice, her mother's names. Even though Carice was an only child, she had lots of friends to play with. As she grew up, she had a white rabbit that she called Peter and loved dearly. At the beginning of the First World War, Carice trained in First Aid and then, from 1915, worked as a translator for the Government Censorship Department. After her mother died, Carice devoted herself to supporting her father. A year after her mother's death, and with her father's consent, Carice became engaged to Samuel Blake, a farmer from Surrey. They were married in January 1922 and she took the name Carice Elgar Blake. They had no children. After the death of her father in 1934 she played a part in the formation of the Elgar Birthplace Trust. Samuel Blake died in 1939, and Carice died in Bristol on 16 July 1970.

Rudyard Kipling

Rudyard Kipling was born on 30 December 1865, in Bombay, India. His father was an artist and worked at the School of Art in Bombay. At the age of 6, Kipling was sent to England to go to school and he lived with a foster family. He was lonely and bullied at home and at school. Kipling took comfort in books and stories and, with few friends, he devoted himself to reading. He returned to India in 1882, where he took a job with the local newspaper. He became very good friends with Wolcott Balestier, and Kipling married his sister, Carrie, in 1892. Kipling and Carrie lived in Vermont, in America, near Carrie's family, and had three children. During this time Kipling wrote *The Jungle Book* (1894) and, by the age of 32, Kipling was the highest-paid writer in the world. In 1916, during the First World War, Kipling wrote an anthology of poems about the sea. Elgar wrote music to accompany four of the poems from the book. However, Kipling's son was lost at sea and, as a result, he banned the music from being played. Kipling died on 18 January 1936.

Pollie Grafton

Susannah Mary, known as 'Pollie', was born on 28 December 1854. She was one of Elgar's elder sisters. She married William Grafton on St George's Day 1879. Edward moved in with his sister and her husband at Loretta Villa, 35 Chestnut Walk, Worcester, in 1879. While living with them, his compositional talents first began to show and he tried to create a new composition or arrangement each weekend. Pollie and Will Grafton signed the marriage register as witnesses at Edward's wedding to Alice when no other relatives attended Elgar's wedding. Elgar called Pollie 'Beak', but she never knew why. She died in 1925.

Alice Stuart-Wortley

Alice Stuart-Wortley was born in 1862. She was the daughter of the successful painter John Millais, who illustrated works by Alfred Tennyson. Alice was known to her family as 'Carrie'. On the 6 January 1886, Alice married Charles Stuart-Wortley, 1st Baron Stuart of Wortley, and a Member of Parliament. She was his second wife. They both loved music and had a grand piano each in their house, where they played Grieg's concertos. Alice and Charles had one daughter, called Clare Euphemia, who was born in 1889. In 1902, they met the Elgars and became close friends. It is rumoured that Elgar fell in love with Alice and she was his inspiration for many pieces of his music. Letters from Elgar to Alice have been found that show the deep affection he had for her. He nicknamed her 'Windflower' as he said that two Alices in his life was confusing. Letters from Windflower to Elgar have been destroyed, possibly by Clare Euphemia. Alice died in 1936.

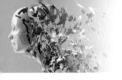

Dame Clara Butt

Dame Clara Ellen Butt, DBE, an English singer, was born on 1 February 1872. In 1880 her family moved from Sussex to Bristol where Clara went to South Bristol High School. Her teachers recognised that Clara was a gifted singer and did much to encourage her. In 1890 she won a scholarship to the Royal College of Music to study singing. She also studied in Paris, Berlin and Italy. Her first public performance was at the Royal Albert Hall in December 1892, when she was still at college. On 26 June 1900, Clara married Kennerley Rumford, a baritone, and they often sang together in concert once they were married. They had two sons and a daughter. Clara was often asked to sing by Queen Victoria, King Edward VII and King George V, and she was the first person to perform *Land of Hope and Glory*. She had a lovely voice and Elgar composed a song with her in mind as the soloist. During the First World War, Clara sang in many concerts for service charities and was awarded the DBE as a result. She died on 23 January 1936, aged 63, at her home in North Stoke, Oxfordshire.

Alfred Tennyson

Born on 6 August 1809, Alfred Tennyson is one of Britain's most famous poets. He was made Poet Laureate in 1850 and kept this position until he died at the age of 83 in 1892. His first work was published at the age of 17 and he went on to Trinity College, Cambridge in 1827 where he joined a secret society called the Cambridge Apostles. Sadly, he was unable to finish his degree as his father died and he had to return home to help his family. Tennyson used a wide range of subjects, including medieval legends and classical myths, domestic situations and observations from nature, as source material for his poetry. His most famous works include the collection *Idylls of the King*, about the life of King Arthur, and *The Lady of Shalott*, about a woman forced to look at life through a mirror. Elgar set music to sections of one of Tennyson's poems, *The Lotos-Eaters*, which is about life on a mythical island. Tennyson rarely travelled, although he did own a home on the Isle of Wight. He is buried at Westminster Abbey, London, in Poets' Corner.

Queen Victoria

Queen Victoria was born on 24 May 1819 and was christened Alexandrina. Victoria was her middle name and she became known as Queen Victoria when she ascended to the throne in 1837, at the age of 18. She reigned for longer than any other British monarch to date, dying in 1901 after over 63 years on the throne. Many poems and works of music were written in her honour and Edward Elgar came to fame after writing a piece to celebrate her Diamond Jubilee. It was called the *Imperial March*. He also wrote other pieces to celebrate her reign. She married her cousin, Prince Albert, who was a German Prince. They had nine children together and she was distraught when Albert died, spending many years in mourning. Victoria marked the fiftieth anniversary of her accession on 20 June 1887 with a banquet to which 50 kings and princes were invited. She was buried in a white dress and her wedding veil and as her coffin was laid to rest next to her beloved Prince Albert, it began to snow.

Lucy Ann Elgar

Lucy Ann Elgar was born on 29 May 1852 in the town of Worcester. She was more commonly known by her nickname 'Loo' and was the eldest of Edward Elgar's sisters. She said she could clearly remember the day he was born. Little is known about Lucy apart from the fact that she got on very well with her brother. Edward chose to live with Lucy and her husband, Charles Pipe, for a while before his own marriage. From what we know, Lucy lived all her life in Worcester and did not travel much, apart from spending some summers at Broadheath Farm, England.

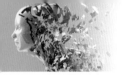

Ann Elgar

Elgar's mother, Ann, was born Ann Greening in 1822. Her father was a farm worker in Weston-under-Penyard in Herefordshire and this meant she had a strong love of the countryside. She didn't go to school very often but learnt to write poetry in her spare time. In 1848, when she was 26, she married William Henry Elgar. They went on to have eight children and one of them was Edward Elgar. Ann helped out in William's music shop in the city of Worcester as a shop assistant. They moved for a short time to the countryside but quickly moved back to Worcester again, where Ann died in 1902.

Sir Arthur Sullivan

In the late 1800s, Sir Arthur Seymour Sullivan was viewed as one of Britain's most promising composers. Born on 13 May 1842, he is most famous as being one half of the composing team, Gilbert and Sullivan. His most famous work is *The Pirates of Penzance* but he wrote many other pieces. He studied in England at the Royal Academy of Music and then in Germany at Leipzig. He travelled extensively, going to Vienna for a while and spending some time in Paris and the South of France. He also spent time in Los Angeles, in America, with his sister's family. He never married. He was knighted by Queen Victoria for his services to music. He was very supportive of the young composer Edward Elgar and, after his death, Elgar wrote about his loss. Some people felt that Sullivan should have written more serious pieces of music and fewer 'comic operas' but Elgar praised him for his talents. As well as working as a composer he tried his hand at teaching music but he did not enjoy this at all. Sullivan died in London, in 1900, of heart failure, having struggled with kidney disease for years.

Creating your database

You'll notice that all of Elgar's friends have a name and a year of birth, so these could become fields for your database. When the name and year of birth relate to say, Clara Butt, these make up a record for Clara.

The fields that you choose for a database record are like an outline sketch of the thing you are modelling; in this case a person. The data that populates the fields forms a full picture from this outline.

You do not need to include everything you know about the person, just the information necessary to solve the problem. If you start out with a different problem you might choose different fields for your database record, which would lead to a different sketch of the same person and therefore a different picture.

For example, you could also use the same raw data to create a register of deaths. You would chose a smaller set of fields and would not include any data about each person's relationship to Elgar. Both databases would be about the same people but they would be different sketches of those people.

Compute-IT

3.1.4   Create a database, using database software, to contain the facts you gathered for 3.1.3 Plan-IT. Use the table below to start off. The names of the fields, which indicate the data required, are at the top of each column. Fill in one record (row) for each person.

FirstName	Surname	YearOf Birth	Gender	Occupation	Relationship ToElgar	LivedAbroad (Y/N)	Place

Think-IT

3.1.5   Which field in the database you created for 3.1.4 Compute-IT could be used for the key field? Would it be better to add a new field rather than use an existing field? Why? And what would you call the new field?

3.2 Using Boolean expressions

Boolean operators and expressions

In order to search a database efficiently you need to be able to construct **Boolean expressions**. These expressions make use of **Boolean operators**.

The result obtained from searching a database will depend on the Boolean operator used as follows:

'x AND y'		only if both x and y are true
'x OR y'	returns a value from the database	if either x or y, or both x and y are true
'NOT x'		if x is false

- If x and y are facts, then 'First name = Susan AND Age = 50' will return all 50-year-old Susans in the database and nothing else.

Think about a database that stores information about every student in a school. It probably contains fields like:

- First name
- Surname
- Tutor group
- Subjects studying
- Commendations

By using Boolean expressions, teachers and support staff can search the database to find, for example, all the students in 9A:

```
Form = 9A
```

Or all the students in Year 10 studying GCSE Geography:

```
Year = 10 AND Subject = Geography
```

Boolean expressions can get quite complex. For example, if you are looking for Year 11 students to take on a Chemistry trip because they have more than ten commendations you would use:

```
Year = 11 AND Subject = Chemistry AND Commendations > 10
```

If you want a list of all the students in 9C as well as any other students that have 25 or more commendations, you would use the following Boolean expression:

```
Form = 9C OR Commendations > = 25
```

Or, if you want all the students in Year 9 except those in 9B and those with less than five commendations, you would use the following Boolean expression:

```
Year = 9 AND Form NOT 9B AND Commendations < 5
```

Think-IT

3.2.1 Draw a Venn diagram and then write a Boolean expression that would find:

   a) all students in Year 10 who do not study Geography

   b) all students in Year 11 who have more than five commendations and who study History

   c) all students in Year 10 who do not study Art but do study Design and Technology.

How do we write Boolean expressions to query a database?

In order to use Boolean expressions in a database you must create a **database query**.

   To write a query we use a query language such as SQL. SQL has certain keywords that the database can understand; words like SELECT, FROM, WHERE, AND, NOT, OR, LIKE, BETWEEN. For example:

> **Key term**
>
> **Database query**: A piece of code that is sent to a database in order to extract information from that database.

```
SELECT * FROM StudentInfo
```

> This query asks the database to return all fields from the database called **StudentInfo**.

```
WHERE Gender = 'M'
```

> This means that only fields for those students that are **Male** should be returned.

```
SELECT FirstName, Surname FROM StudentInfo
```

> This means return just the **FirstName** and **Surname** fields from the database called **StudentInfo**.

```
WHERE Gender = 'F' AND Commendations > 10
```

> This means that only fields for those students that are female and have more than 10 commendations should be returned.

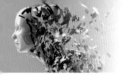

What if you only have a vague idea about the person you are looking for? If you are looking for a student whose surname sounds like 'Johnson' but you don't know how it is spelt (it could be 'Johnson', 'Jonson', 'Johnstone' etc.) the following SQL command will pick out students with similar surnames:

```
Surname LIKE J%s%on%
```

The database will look for students whose surname starts with 'J' and includes 's' and 'on', and give you a list.

LIKE is an SQL command that uses wildcards to locate data, for example:

- LIKE %S will find anything ending in S.
- LIKE %S% will find anything with an S anywhere in the word.
- LIKE S% will find anything starting with S.

Compute-IT

3.2.2 Look at the following SQL queries. Read the descriptions of Elgar's friends and family on pages 37–44. Pick two of the following queries, and work out which of Elgar's friends would be returned in each case.

a) SELECT * FROM Elgar's Friends

WHERE Gender = 'M'

b) SELECT * FROM Elgar's Friends

WHERE LivedAbroad = 'Y'

c) SELECT * FROM Elgar's Friends

WHERE Occupation = 'Musician'

d) SELECT * FROM Elgar's Friends

WHERE Gender = 'M'

AND Place LIKE '%Leipzig%'

e) SELECT * FROM Elgar's Friends

WHERE LivedAbroad = 'Y'

AND Place NOT India

f) SELECT Name FROM Elgar's Friends

WHERE Gender = 'M'

OR Gender = 'F'

AND YearOfBirth BETWEEN 1840 AND 1860

Your second clue is:

The person you are looking for lived abroad.

Compute-IT

3.2.3 Search the database you created for 3.1.4 Compute-IT, creating queries using the database query wizard or SQL to answer the following questions. Remember, if you get stuck, use the Help facility that comes with the database software that you are using to help you.

a) Find all the men.

b) Find all the male writers.

c) Find all the women.

d) Find all the women that have lived abroad.

e) What was Billy Reed's occupation?

f) What relation to Elgar was the shop assistant?

g) List all the friends who have 'ed' in their name somewhere.

h) Which of Elgar's colleagues were born in the 1860s?

i) Find all of Elgar's blood relations.

j) Find Elgar's colleagues who were not singers or writers. You'll need to think carefully about this!

k) Find all of Elgar's sisters who have lived abroad.

3.3 Solving the clues to find the subject of Enigma Variation XIII

How good is our database?

A database is only as good as the data in it. Common problems with databases include:

- Inaccurate data: data with spelling mistakes or just incorrect data, such as an old address.
- **Redundant data**: duplicated data, where the same data is stored more than once, wasting space and increasing the chance of mistakes being made. For example, if a doctor holds the name and address of each member of a family separately they may forget to update the address for one family member if the family moves.

If we use a database containing inaccurate or redundant data we may not extract the correct records when we query the database and this could have serious consequences, for example in the case of criminal or medical records. A smaller database is also quicker to search.

Checking the accuracy of a database

There are two methods for checking the accuracy of a database: **verification** and **validation**. When you verify the data in a database, you check to see that it matches the data as it was originally captured. For example, you look back at the questionnaire or the form that was filled in. 'Validation' is the name given to a set of automatic checks that a computer conducts on the data in a database to ensure that it is sensible, reasonable, complete and lies between given boundaries.

> **Key term**
>
> **Redundant data**: Duplicated data, when the data in a database is stored more than once. It can lead to inconsistency of the database and should be avoided wherever possible.

> **Key terms**
>
> **Verification**: The process of checking that the data in a database matches the data as it was originally captured.
>
> **Validation**: A set of automatic checks that a computer conducts on the data in a database to ensure that it is sensible, reasonable, complete and lies between given boundaries.

The standard validation checks include:

Check	Description
Existence	Checks that the data being entered exists in the database. For example, that the database has a field for Student Id.
Format	Checks that the correct format has been used. For example, dd/mm/yy for date of birth.
Length	Checks that the text is less than a given number of characters. For example, that no more than 11 characters are provided for a telephone number.
Presence	Checks that required information has been entered and the field is not left blank.
Range	Checks that a number falls in the correct range. For example, that a number > 18 is entered into the Age field if the person must be over 18.
Type	Checks that the data entered is the correct type. For example, that letters and not numbers are entered.

It is important to remember that validation cannot check that the data is correct, only that it is as expected or specified.

Lookup tables and relational databases

To avoid duplication and keep the memory required to store a database as small as possible, we can abbreviate some of the data as we enter it, although we need to be careful that we don't introduce errors when we do this. For example:

- 'Yes' becomes 'Y'
- 'No' becomes 'N'
- 'Female' becomes 'F'
- 'Male' becomes 'M'.

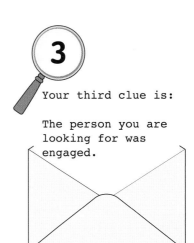

Your third clue is:

The person you are looking for was engaged.

Think-IT

3.3.1   Look at the database of Elgar's friends you created for 3.1.4 Compute-IT. Which fields could be abbreviated and what could they be abbreviated to?

A lookup table can be added to a relational database to store the abbreviations we use and can tell the computer what they stand for. With relational databases the data is stored in separate tables rather than one big table as in a flat file database. The tables are then linked together using primary and **foreign keys**.

Compute-IT

3.3.2 Redesign the database you created for 3.1.4 Compute-IT as a relational database.

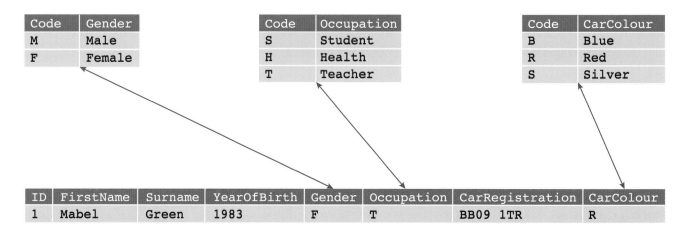

Code	Gender
M	Male
F	Female

Code	Occupation
S	Student
H	Health
T	Teacher

Code	CarColour
B	Blue
R	Red
S	Silver

ID	FirstName	Surname	YearOfBirth	Gender	Occupation	CarRegistration	CarColour
1	Mabel	Green	1983	F	T	BB09 1TR	R

▲ A database using lookup tables

Challenge

Nobody knows the subject of Variation XIII of Edward Elgar's *Enigma Variations*, although there are clues. Your challenge is to discover who this piece of music is about by following the clues and constructing and interrogating a database.

You are about to discover the answer to this question. You just need to discover some more clues as to their identity.

Compute-IT

3.3.3 Use the clues scattered throughout this unit and the last clue below to search the database you created for 3.1.4 Compute-IT to narrow down the list of Elgar's friends and find the person to whom he dedicated Enigma Variation XIII.

Your fourth clue is coded using the PigPen cypher. The Pigpen cypher was used in the 18th century by the Freemasons to code their records to keep them secret. The cypher works by substituting each letter for a symbol.

The PigPen cypher key ▶

Think-IT

3.3.4 It is important to document discoveries so that other people trust your findings. Prepare a poster, a newspaper article, a radio show or a short film about the journey that led you to discover who *Enigma Variation XIII* was written about. You should include:

- a description of your database: how it was constructed and the data it contains
- the queries you used when you received each clue and the results returned by your database
- a brief biography of the person *Enigma Variation XIII* was written about.

Unit 4 Searching

4.1 Linear search

Going from door to door

Often the actions we perform on a computer, such as finding a name in an email address book or finding a computer file involve looking for things or 'searching'.

Think-IT

4.1.1 Imagine you are looking for a long-lost friend. You know the street they live on but don't know the house number. How might you go about finding which house they live in?

If we're looking for a long-lost friend and know the street they live on but not the house number, we have no choice but to start knocking on doors until we find our friend. It doesn't matter which order we knock on the doors but it is easier to keep track of the doors we haven't yet knocked on if, for example, we start by knocking on the door of house number one. If our friend doesn't live there we move onto the next house. We repeat this until we find our friend. Here is an algorithm to represent this.

```
Start at house 1
WHILE we haven't found our friend:
    knock on the door and see who lives there
    IF it's not our friend THEN
        Move to the next door
    END IF
END WHILE
We are now at our friend's house
```

Plan-IT

4.1.3 If we get to the end of the street and haven't found our friend then we can conclude that he doesn't live on the street after all. Amend the pseudocode on the left so it either gives the house number our friend lives at or states he does not live on that street.

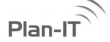

Plan-IT

4.1.2 Create a flowchart to represent the algorithm above.

We call this approach – starting at the beginning of a list and checking it item by item – a **linear search**.

There are eleven houses in the street where our friend lives. If we are lucky we will only need to knock on one door, if we are really unlucky we will need to knock on eleven.

Key term

Linear search: A method of searching where you start at the beginning of a list and check it item by item.

Think-IT

4.1.4 Have you ever played the game Battleships? The game is played on four grids, two for each player. Each player arranges ships and records their opponent's shots on one grid and records their own shots on the second grid. The aim of the game is to guess the squares occupied by a ship and sink it.

Devise a strategy to win at Battleships.

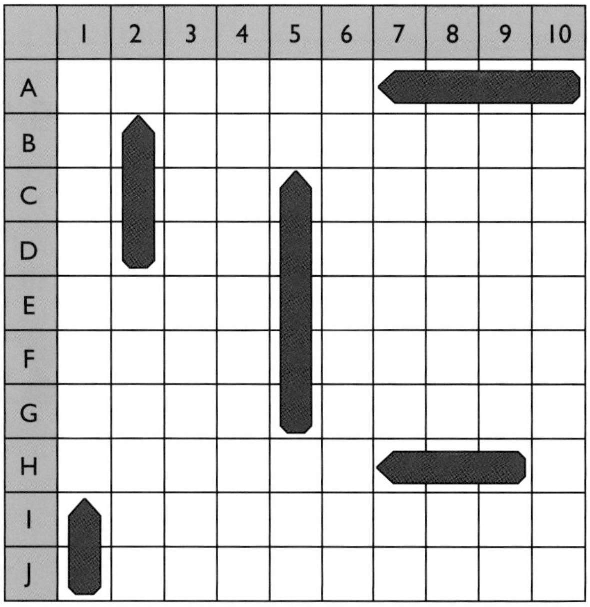

4.2 Implementing a linear search

Arrays and lists

The first thing to consider when implementing a search on a computer is what we will use to store the data that is being searched. In programming we use something called a data structure to store items of data. For linear search we need a data structure that stores a collection of items sequentially. There are two common forms of sequential data structures, arrays and lists. Some programming languages, such as BASIC, use arrays and others, such as Python and Scratch, use lists.

You will recall that arrays and lists store data with a numbered index for each position in the sequence of items. Here is an array we shall call 'Houses' representing the names of people living in eleven houses.

1	Lynwood
2	Lily
3	Kimberley
4	Jeremy
5	Hoyt
6	Dalton
7	Franklyn
8	Vasiliki
9	Adrian
10	Tori
11	Ahmed

Finding one item

In most programming languages we can get the value of an item in an array using 'arrayname[index]'. So `Houses[4]` is Jeremy. In Scratch we use the 'Item X of' block after we have created a list.

This is how we select the fourth item in a list called 'Houses' in Scratch 2.0. ▶

Think-IT

4.2.1 **a)** How do we get to item 3 in an array or list?

b) How do we get to item 6 in an array or list?

c) How do we get to item 'i' in an array or list?

Using a loop

Now we know how to find one item in the array or list, we need to think about how we go through the array or list one item at a time. We can do this using a loop. Pseudocode for a program to print out every name in an array is shown on the right.

```
x=1
WHILE x<= Length of Houses
     PRINT(houses[x])
     x=x+1
END WHILE
```

Finding a particular item

Of course with linear search we don't want to print out every name. We want to find and print one particular name. So let's remove PRINT(houses[x]) and add a line creating a variable to store the name of the person we are looking for. This is shown on the right.

```
x=1
lookingFor="Dalton"
WHILE x<= Length of Houses
     x=x+1
END WHILE
```

Instead of searching all the names, we want to work through them until we find the person we are looking for.

Plan-IT

4.2.2 Amend the pseudocode above so the loop repeats while the person living at the house doesn't match the person you are looking for.

4.2.3 Complete the pseudocode you amended for 4.2.2 Plan-IT to output the message, 'lookingFor' lives at house number 'x' . For example, Dalton lives at house number 3.

Compute-IT

4.2.4 Use the algorithm you developed for 4.2.2 Plan-IT and 4.2.3 Plan-IT to create a linear search program in a graphical programming language. It should ask for a name and then search for that name in a list.

4.2.5 Modify the program you wrote for 4.2.4 Compute-IT so that it deals with searching for a name that isn't in the list.

4.3 Programming a binary search

Ahmed and Bianca are playing a number guessing game. Ahmed tells Bianca that he can guarantee that if she thinks of a number between 0 and 1000 he can guess the number she has thought of by asking ten or fewer 'higher or lower questions'.

Think-IT

4.3.1 Ahmed guessed Bianca's number in nine guesses. How could he be so confident he would get it in under 10 guesses?

Key term

Binary search: A method of searching where the search splits the part of the list being searched in two with each check.

Ahmed managed to guess Bianca's number using a process known as **binary search**. Binary search splits the part of the list being searched in two with each check.

To perform a binary search we need to set the boundaries of where we are trying to search. If we think back to Ahmed and Bianca's guessing game, we know the number is greater than or equal to 0 and less than or equal to 1000. We can store these numbers as the 'Lower bound' and the 'Upper bound' respectively.

We also want the halfway point between the two. We can calculate this by adding the upper bound to the lower bound and dividing by two:

(0 + 1000) / 2 = 500

so our midpoint is 500. We can think of this on a number line:

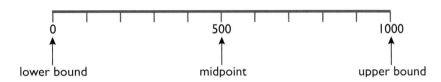

We check to see if the midpoint is the number we are looking for. If it is, then we can stop. If the midpoint is too high we can ignore everything bigger than the midpoint. This means the number before the midpoint becomes our new upper bound:

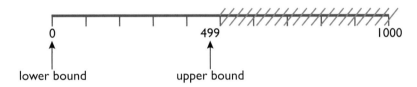

On the other hand if the midpoint is too low we can ignore everything smaller than the midpoint. This means the number after the midpoint becomes our new lower bound:

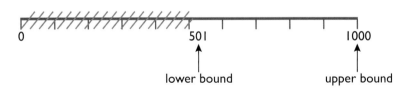

In either of these cases, we can then calculate our new midpoint and repeat the process until we find the number we are looking for.

Plan-IT

4.3.2 Write a set of instructions for someone who has never seen Ahmed's number guessing game before, telling them how to carry it out.

Compute-IT

4.3.3 Write a program in a graphical programming language to perform Ahmed's number guessing game.

Think-IT

4.3.4 Binary search can only be used in certain circumstances. When can binary search not be used?

Think-IT

4.4.1 If the item we are looking for is the very first item in a list, which will give a quicker result, linear search or binary search? How about if the item we are looking for is the very last item in the list?

4.4 Comparing a binary search to a linear search

There are some circumstances when linear search will return better results and some circumstances when binary search will return better results. What is most important is which method will find the solution quickest **most** of the time. The fewer locations we have to check before finding the value we are looking for, the quicker the search time.

Which is quicker?

For both types of search, the best-case scenario is that we find the item we are looking for in the first location we check. But what about the worst-case scenario?

Using a linear search, the worst-case scenario is that the value we are looking for is at the end of the list. For example, if the list is 15 items long then we will need to check 15 items.

For a binary search the worst-case scenario is that we have to discount all the items aside from the one we are looking for. For example, if we look at this list of 15 letters to search for 'K', we would pick 'H' as the middle point and discount half the list:

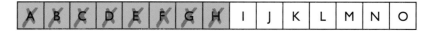

Next we would check 'L' and discount 'L' to 'O':

Then we would check 'J' and discount 'I' and 'J':

Finally we would check the remaining item, 'K', and find our solution:

We would have found our item after four checks.

To calculate the worst-case scenario for a binary search we have to count how many times we have to halve the size of the part of the list we are searching to get to one or lower. For the example above, the calculation would be:

$$15 \div 2 = 7.5 \div 2 = 3.75 \div 2 = 1.875 \div 2 = 0.9375$$

We have to divide by 2 **four** times to get to 1 or lower, making the worst-case scenario four checks.

The item we are searching for in a large data set may be anywhere in a list or an array. We may be lucky and find the item quickly or we may end up with the worst-case scenario. We can see this in an experiment by repeatedly searching a large data file for different items and counting the number of iterations we need to find each item.

Compute-IT

4.4.2 Go to **www.hoddereducation.co.uk/ compute-it/search**

This web page generates a list of schools and you can specify how many schools you want on the list by inputting a number between 1 and 3000 into the 'Number of schools (1-3000):' box. When you press 'Run Search' a school is picked at random from the list and a linear search and a binary search are performed to find the chosen school in the list. You are presented with the number of times the program had to check the list to find the school.

a) Choose the number of schools you would like to include in your list – somewhere between 30 and 3000 – and use the web page to find out the number of checks required by a linear search and a binary search to find an item in a list of that length.

b) The position of the school in the list will affect the result, so repeat part **a** several times and work out the average number of checks required by a linear search and a binary search to find an item in a list of your chosen length. Record your findings in a spreadsheet.

c) Now choose a different number of schools – again somewhere between 30 and 3000 – to include in your list and work out the average number of

checks required by a linear search and a binary search to find an item in a list of your chosen length. Record your findings in your spreadsheet.

d) Repeat part **c** eight times so that you have data for ten different list lengths. Record all your findings in your spreadsheet.

e) Plot the data from your spreadsheet on a graph like the one below.

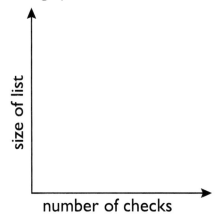

f) Are there instances where a linear search performs better than a binary search?

g) What is the lowest number of checks needed for a linear search and a binary search for 30 and 3000 schools?

h) What is the highest number of checks needed for a linear search and binary search of 30 and 3000 schools?

i) What do you notice about the results?

4.5 Implementing a binary search

We have looked at how to perform a binary search on a number line but we often want to apply it to an array or a list, just like we did with linear search.

Imagine, once again, that we're searching for a friend in a street but this time everyone lives in alphabetical order of first name. For example, Alan might live in the first house on the street, Afzal lives in the second house on the street and so on, until we get to Zoe who lives at the last house on the street. We want to find our friend Hamish but don't know the number of the house he lives at. We could perform a linear search but the fact that everyone lives in alphabetical order gives us a better option: a binary search.

Initially, the lower bound will be first house on the street and the upper bound will be the last house on the street. In the case of the diagram below, houses 1 and 11.

We can calculate the number of the house in the middle, house 6.

We can check who lives in house 6. `Houses[6]` is Paul.

Think-IT

4.5.1 Look back to pages 58–59.

What calculation is performed on the lower bound '1' and upper bound '11' to get the midpoint of '6'?

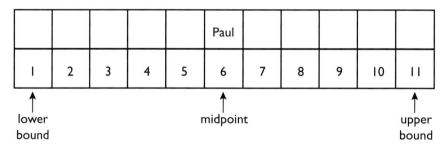

Paul is not the person we are looking for so we compare the result, 'Paul', to the name we are looking for, 'Hamish'. 'Paul' comes after 'Hamish' in the alphabet so we know that Hamish must live somewhere between Paul's house and the start of the street. We can therefore ignore Paul and all the houses after his: the upper bound becomes the midpoint – 1.

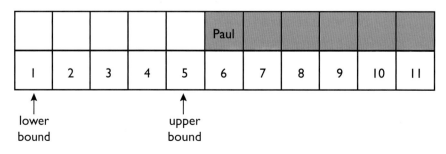

Next we go to the house at the middle point between the lower and upper bounds using the same formula you developed for 4.5.1 Think-IT. This should give you the midpoint of '3'. `Houses[3]` is Bea. 'Bea' is before 'Hamish' in the alphabet so we can discount Bea and all the houses before Bea's house. This means our new lower bound is midpoint + 1.

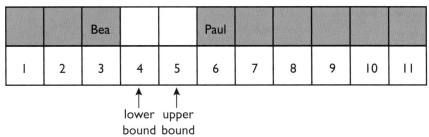

Repeating the process again we get a midpoint of 4.5, which we round up to 5. We find out that Naz lives at Number 5.

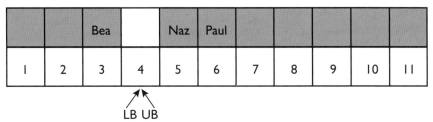

Finally we have the upper and lower bounds pointing to the same location. We check this and find Hamish.

		Bea	Hamish	Naz	Paul					
1	2	3	4	5	6	7	8	9	10	11

Think-IT

4.5.2 What could we have deduced if Hamish hadn't been at Number 4?

Plan-IT

4.5.3 Complete this algorithm for a binary search:

```
searchedName="Hamish"

upperBound=endOfList
lowerBound=startOfList
midPoint=[INSERT FORMULA FROM 4.5.1 THINK-IT]
WHILE Houses[midPoint]!=searchedName
        IF Houses[midPoint]<searchedName THEN
                [?]Bound=midPoint[?]1
        ELSE
                [?]Bound=midPoint[?]1
        END IF
        midPoint=[INSERT FORMULA FROM 4.5.1 THINK-IT]
END WHILE
PRINT("Hamish lives at house number"+midPoint)
```

Plan-IT

4.5.4 If the person you are looking for isn't at the location where the upper and lower bounds meet then they are not in the list. Adapt the algorithm in 4.5.3 Plan-IT so it takes this into account.

4.6 Creating a spell checker

Challenge

Now you understand how to program a search algorithm, you are ready to take on the challenge for this unit, to create a spell checker.

Most word-processing programs have built-in spell checkers, but how do they work and how can you use your understanding of searching to create your own spell checker?

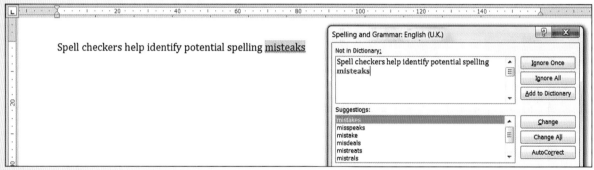

▲ Spell checkers help identify potential spelling mistakes.

To work, a spell checker needs a list of correctly spelt words. We call this list a **dictionary**. It should be not be confused with the traditional use of the word dictionary. This list contains words but not definitions.

The spell checker looks at the word the user has entered. It then checks the dictionary to see if it can find the word the user has entered. If the spell checker can find the word it knows it has been spelt correctly. If, however, it can't find the word in the dictionary it assumes it has been spelt incorrectly. It goes through this process for every word in the document it is checking.

Key term

Dictionary: A list of all the words known to the application in alphabetical order.

Think-IT

4.6.1 When might a spell checker say a correctly spelt word is wrong? When might it not spot an incorrectly spelt word?

In order to check the dictionary, a spell checker performs a search.

Think-IT

4.6.2 Which algorithm do you think a spell checker uses to search the dictionary, a binary search or a linear search?

Think-IT

4.6.4 How effective would a spell checker be on the poem below?

Compute-IT

4.6.3 Create a spell checker in a graphical programming language, which checks the spelling of 17-letter words, or create a spell checker in a text-based programming language, which checks the spelling in a text document. Remember to design your solution before you begin coding and, as part of the design process, decide whether your spell checker is going to perform a binary search or a linear search.

Candidate for a Pullet Surprise

I have a spelling checker.
It came with my PC.
It plane lee marks four my revue
Miss steaks aye can knot sea.

Eye ran this poem threw it,
Your sure reel glad two no.
Its vary polished inn it's weigh.
My checker tolled me sew.

A checker is a bless sing,
It freeze yew lodes of thyme.
It helps me right awl stiles two reed,
And aides me when aye rime.

Each frays come posed up on my screen
Eye trussed too bee a joule.
The checker pours o'er every word
To cheque sum spelling rule.

Bee fore a veiling checkers
Hour spelling mite decline,
And if we're lacks oar have a laps,
We wood bee maid too wine.

Butt now bee cause my spelling
Is checked with such grate flare,
Their are know faults with in my cite,
Of nun eye am a wear.

Now spelling does knot phase me,
It does knot bring a tier.
My pay purrs awl due glad den
With wrapped words fare as hear.

To rite with care is quite a feet
Of witch won should bee proud,
And wee mussed dew the best wee can,
Sew flaws are knot aloud.

Sow ewe can sea why aye dew prays
Such soft wear four pea seas,
And why eye brake in two avers
Buy righting want too pleas.

Dr Jerrold Zar, 29 June 1992

Getting down and dirty with networks

5.1 The internet protocol suite and the application layer

Communication protocols

For two computers to communicate with each other, they have to follow a set of rules. These are called **communication protocols**. These protocols carry out different jobs at different levels of abstraction. For the internet they are grouped into four different layers:

- Layer 1: Application
- Layer 2: Door-to-door transport
- Layer 3: Internet layer
- Layer 4: Network layer

Together these layers are called the **internet protocol suite**.

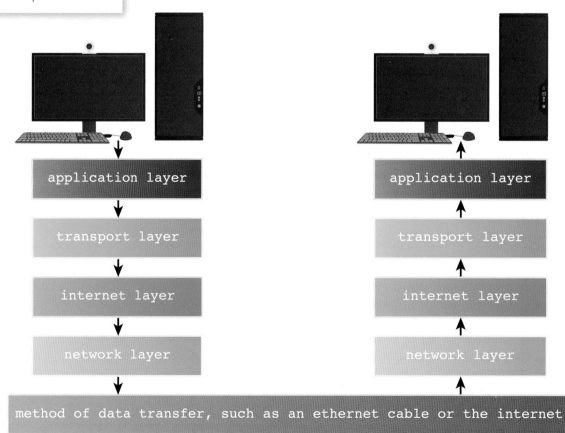

▲ The four layers of the internet protocol suite

The application layer

The first layer, the application layer, is made up of standard communication services that applications, such as web browsers, can use to communicate with the second layer. The application layer presents the abstraction of direct application-to-application communication. For example, from the perspective of two user email applications, it is as if an email message is sent from the sender's email application to the recipient's email application. In fact the message is passed down from the sender's application layer, through the other layers, across the physical network and then back up through the layers on the recipient's side of the communication. Each layer performs the tasks necessary at that layer to provide the ultimate abstraction of direct application-to-application communication.

The transport layer

The door-to-door transport layer deals with the sending and receiving of data over a network. It receives data from the layer above it, divides it into packets and then passes them on to their next destination within the Local Area Network (LAN) or beyond. It also reassembles the individual packets it receives.

The internet and network layers

The internet layer handles the logical addressing and management of data packets. The network layer contains the drivers and the hardware that are used to transfer data from source to destination.

Application layer protocols

There are a number of different application layer protocols, including SMTP, IMAP, POP and FTP.

SMTP

Simple Mail Transfer Protocol is the communication protocol used for sending emails over the internet. It was created in 1982 and is used by all of the major email systems, including Gmail, Hotmail and Yahoo!.

You use a graphical user interface to write your email, but when you press 'Send' SMTP takes your email and breaks it into strings of text and uses labels to identify certain parts. These labels and strings of text are used to form an email header. The email is then sent to your mail server, which authenticates your username and password,

> **Key term**
>
> **SMTP (Simple Mail Transfer Protocol)**: The communication protocol used for sending emails over the internet.

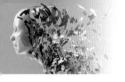

before using the information in the header to look up where the email should be sent and passing it on to the recipient's mail server so that it can be delivered.

x-store-info:sbeck12QZROXo7W1D5ZcVBK1Phj2jX/
Authentication-Results: hotmail.com; spf=pass (sender IP is 00.00.000.000; identity alignment result Is pass and alignment mode is relaxed)
X-SID-PRA: ilovecomputing@hotmail.org
X-AUTH-Result: PASS
X-SID-Result: PASS
X-Message-Status: n:n
X-Message-Delivery:Vj0xLjE7dXM9MDtsPTA7YT0x00Q9MTHRD0xO1NDTD0x
X-Message-Info:
    iTOHNJf19IjHGaTN8CSarW4/emvdGxLuhMq5Ba4y+63k6ylOVW6VeNA7j%pIjMI0MMkYQ
    Q3MVpZOHxAClrTqubJLGS05Fv7gnBqyPOYYXExD+2p4aVaS+b2lhSX1
Received: from blu0-omc4-s27.blu0hotmail.com([00.00.000.000]) by COL0-MC6-F5.Col0.hotmail.com with
    Microsoft SMTPSVC(6.6.6666.6666); Fri, 25 Apr 2014 04:39:07 −0700
Received: from BLU175-Wl6 ([11.11.111.111]) by blu0-omc-s27.blu0.hotmail.com with Microsoft
    SMTPSVC (6.6.6666.6666); Fri, 25 Apr 2014 04:39:07 −0700
X-TMN: [2NtaFtjRj/h6yxl06YHqqGA2+KeH1SPo]
X-originating-Email: [ilovecomputing@hotmail.org]
Message-ID: <BLU175-W166827A14F000AA3599ED4DF5A0@phx.gbl>
Return-path: ilovecomputing@hotmail.org
Content-Type: multipart/alternative; boundary="_e72cf222-b70f-42af-9beb-f8f4f3b37e72_"
From: Carl Turland <ilovecomputing@hotmail.org>
To: George Rouse <computersciencegeek@outlook.org>
Subject: Hello!
Date: Fri, 25 Apr 2014 12:39:06 +0100
Importance: Normal
MIME-Version: 1.0
X-OriginalArrivalTime: 25 Apr 2014 11:39:06.0675 (UTC)
    FILETIME=[F734E830:01CF607A]
-- e72cf222-b70f-42af-9beb-f8f4f3b37e72_
Content-Type: text/plain; charset="iso-8859-1"
Content-Transfer-Encoding: quoted-printable
Hello!

▲ An example of an email header

Think-IT

5.1.1   Look through the email header. Can you identify who sent the email, who received it and what the message was?

Compute-IT

5.1.2   Look at a web-based email account and find out how to view an email header. Then try and trace the origin of one email using suitable software or a web-based tool which you can find by searching for 'email source' using a search engine. Note: Some webmail providers now hide some of the information in an email header so not all emails are traceable. If this happens, you will be given a warning that information is missing and you will not be able to retrieve all of it.

IMAP vs POP

IMAP (Internet Message Access Protocol) and **POP (Post Office Protocol)** are the two most popular protocols used to retrieve emails from a mail server. However, they do not operate in the same manner. In normal operation, an IMAP client downloads a copy of an email message (or the header information about the message) and the original message is kept on the server. This means that other IMAP clients can download a copy of the same message. In contrast, when a POP client downloads a message it is removed from the server and the POP email client application is responsible for storing the message locally.

IMAP is the most popular protocol used to access emails these days. This is because many of us access our emails from a number of different devices – from our mobile phones, our desktop computers, our laptops and our tablets – so downloading our emails to one device using POP gives an incomplete view of our emails on different devices.

The benefits of IMAP are:

- Your emails can be accessed anywhere on any device.
- It means there is a copy of your emails on the mail server.
- It is faster to check your emails as the content is only downloaded when you view the email.
- You choose whether you wish to download any attachments.
- Changes made to your emails, when you delete or copy for example, are automatically updated on the mail server.

The disadvantages of IMAP are:

- You are relying on your email provider to look after your emails.
- It is slower to search for an email.
- It is harder to backup your emails locally.

> ### Key terms
>
> **IMAP (Internet Message Access Protocol):** A protocol used to retrieve emails from a mail server and leave a copy of the email on the server, allowing multiple clients to access the same email.
>
> **POP (Post Office Protocol):** A protocol to download emails from a mail server. When downloaded the emails are removed from the server and stored locally.

▲ An email application using IMAP on a mobile phone

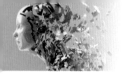

POP does have its benefits:

- You can access the emails that you have downloaded even when you do not have an internet connection.
- It is much easier to backup and archive your emails locally.
- You have control over, and responsibility for the security of, your emails once they have been downloaded.
- It is faster to search emails that are stored locally.

The disadvantages of POP are:

- It is difficult to access your emails on multiple devices.
- All your emails can be lost if your hard drive becomes corrupted.
- All emails, which could include spam and potential viruses, are downloaded to your computer.
- Emails are normally automatically deleted on the email server unless set up to keep a copy.

Think-IT

5.1.3 Find out which protocol the app on your phone is currently using to access your emails.

a) How did you find this out?

b) Do you have the option of changing the protocol it uses?

c) Which protocol do you think suits you best and why?

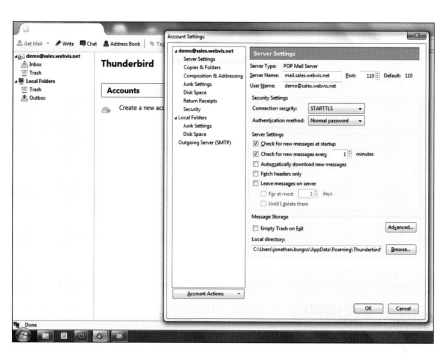

▲ An email application using POP3 (POP version 3) on a desktop computer

FTP

FTP (File Transfer Protocol) is the protocol used to transfer files from one computer to another computer over a network. This may be a local area network or the internet. It is often used by web developers to upload web page files, such as the HTML source code, from their local computer to the server which is hosting their website. To transfer files from one computer to another you need access to both computers so, to send something using the FTP protocol, you will need a username and password to log on to the receiving computer.

Most people who use FTP use a graphical FTP client such as FileZilla. Graphical FTP clients simplify the process by allowing you to drag and drop files on or off the receiving computer. Alternatively, you can use a web browser or a command-line interface.

> ### Key term
>
> **FTP (File Transfer Protocol)**: A protocol used to transfer files from one computer to another computer over a network.

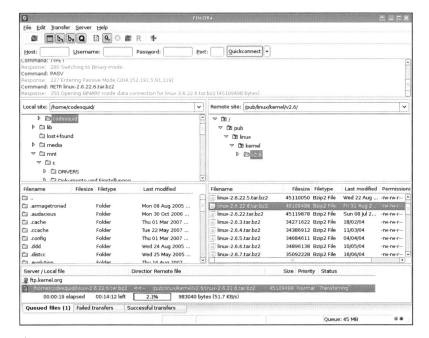

▲ FileZilla is an example of a graphical FTP client.

▲ Using the command line to FTP

5.2 Networks

IP addresses on networks

The lowest layer of the internet protocol suite, the network layer, is known as the physical layer and consists of the devices used to access the network; devices like the Network Interface Card or NIC.

Each device on a home network is assigned a private IP address, which is only used within the Local Area Network (LAN). When you access the internet all the devices on a LAN use one public IP address that is assigned to your modem–router by your Internet Service Provider (ISP).

▲ A Network Interface Card with two ethernet ports

172 . 16 . 254 . 1

10101100.00010000.11111110.00000001

▲ IPv4 addresses are 32-bit numbers.

2001 : 0DB8 : AC10 : FE01

10000000000001:0000110110111000:1010110000010000:1111111000000001

▲ The newer IPv6 addresses are 128-bit numbers.

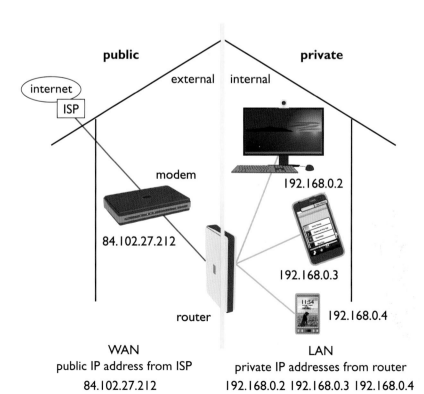

public   private

external   internal

internet
ISP

modem

192.168.0.2

84.102.27.212

192.168.0.3

router   192.168.0.4

WAN   LAN
public IP address from ISP   private IP addresses from router
84.102.27.212   192.168.0.2 192.168.0.3 192.168.0.4

A LAN, where every device ▶ is assigned a private IP address, and a WAN, where all the devices on a LAN connect to the internet using the same public IP address

You can use the command line interface or the network tools available on your operating system to find your private IP address.

```
C:\Users\Home>ipconfig

Windows IP Configuration


Ethernet adapter Local Area Connection:

   Connection-specific DNS Suffix  . :
   Link-local IPv6 Address . . . . . : fe80::7424:e52b:83ae:ecff%11
   IPv4 Address. . . . . . . . . . . : 192.168.0.3
   Subnet Mask . . . . . . . . . . . : 255.255.255.0
   Default Gateway . . . . . . . . . : 192.168.0.1
```

▲ How to find your private IP address using the Windows command line interface

To find your public IP address you can use any number of websites online. Search for 'what is my public IP address'.

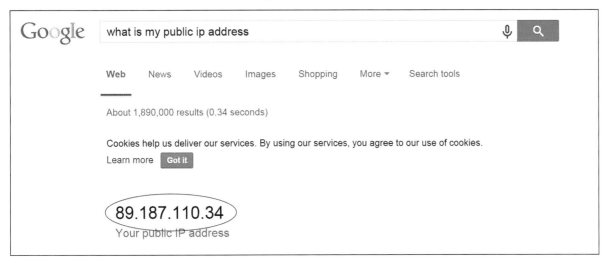

▲ How to find your public IP address online

Think-IT

5.2.1 Find out the public and, if you are also connected to a LAN, the local (private) IP address of the devices you have which are connected to the internet. This may be your computer, your laptop, your mobile phone or your tablet for example.

Your public IP address gives away information about you and the device you are using to connect to the internet. For example, using your IP address it is possible to establish your rough location, the Internet Service Provider you use, the operating system you are running and even the colour depth and screen resolution of your device.

The majority of home internet users will have a dynamic public IP address, meaning it will change regularly. How often it changes will depend on your ISP. Servers hosting websites have to have a static IP address so they can be found on the internet easily. This is why your IP address may change from day to day, but a website like **www.google.co.uk** will always have the same IP address.

🔍 **news.sky.com - IP Tracing and IP Tracking**

Want to trace or track an IP Address, host, or website easily? With our highly reliable IP Address Location Database, you can get detailed information on any **IP Address** anywhere in the world. Results include detailed IP address location, name of ISP, netspeed/speed of internet connection, and more.

news.sky.com
Location of the
Host IP address
23.3.13.208:
Cambridge in
United States

▲ Sometimes the location of a server hosting a website may not be where you expected! In this image we can see that the server is located in Cambridge in the United States of America. This image was returned from the website www.ip-address.com.

Compute-IT

5.2.2 a) Copy and complete the table, finding out about the IP addresses of the following websites:

Domain name	Public IP address	Country in which the server that hosts the website is situated	City in which the server that hosts the website is situated
www.bbc.co.uk			
www.twitter.co.uk			
www.google.co.uk			
www.google.co.in			
www.thepiratebay.org			

b) Where is the server that hosts your public IP address? How many routers are there between you and your public IP address?

MAC addresses

Any IP address assigned to a device can be changed quite easily. However, there is an address assigned to every NIC (Network Interface Card) that is permanent and cannot be changed. This address is the **MAC address** and it is known by the device that assigns the NIC its private IP address, usually your network router. 'MAC' stands for 'Media Access Control'.

Key term

MAC (Media Access Control) address: A unique identifier assigned to Network Interface Cards.

```
C:\Users\Home>getmac

Physical Address      Transport Name
===================   ===========================================
BC-5F-F4-8A-EF-47     \Device\Tcpip_{039AE566-FE96-48C7-8E84-DC594A40D4B1}
```

▲ The MAC address (called the 'Physical Address' here) is accessed using the command 'getmac' in the Windows command line interface.

A MAC address is made up of 48 bits. The first six characters of the MAC address identify the manufacturer of the NIC. The last six characters are unique. For example:

    mm-mm-mm-uu-uu-uu

or

    mm:mm:mm:uu:uu:uu

where m is the manufacturer code and u is the unique code.

There are a number of websites that can be used to identify the manufacturer code part of a MAC address.

Think-IT

5.2.3 Find the MAC addresses for all your devices that have an NIC. This could include your computer, your laptop, your mobile phone or your tablet.

English | Русский | Deutsch | Español

◀ A screenshot from www.adminsub.net/mac-address-finder showing that LG Electronics makes the devices with a MAC address beginning BC:F5:AC

| IPv4 Subnet Calculator | Password Generator/Decryptor | MAC Address Finder |

MAC Address Finder

MAC address or vendor: `BC:F5:AC`   [Search]

Enter **first 6 characters** or **full** MAC address. Or search by Vendor name, e.g. **cisco** or **apple**

Database updated - February 11, 2014

Search results for "bcf5ac"

MAC	Vendor
BCF5AC	LG Electronics

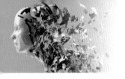

Hexadecimal

Usually MAC addresses are shown in **hexadecimal**. Hexadecimal (or 'hex' for short) has a base of 16. It works in the same way as binary, which has a base of 2, and decimal, which has a base of 10, but it has 16 possible numbers (0–15). We already have symbols to represent the numbers 0 to 9 but need six more symbols for the numbers 10 to 15. We use the symbol 'A' to represent 10, 'B' to represent 11, up to 'F' to represent 15.

0, 1, 2, 3, 4, 5, 6, 7, 8, 9, A, B, C, D, E, F

Converting hexadecimal to decimal

The column values in hexadecimal are, from right to left, 1s, 16s, 256s (16 × 16), etc. and we can use a table to illustrate how to convert the hexadecimal number 'B7' to decimal (base 10).

Column value	16	1
Hexadecimal	B	7

The first column has a value of 1 and we have 7 of them:

```
7 × 1 = 7
```

The second column has a value of 16 and we have B (11) of them:

```
11 × 16 = 176
```

If we add these totals together we end up with the value in decimal:

```
7 + 176 = 183
```

$$B7_{16} = 183_{10}$$

The small subscript numbers show which base the number is in.

Converting decimal to hexadecimal

To convert a decimal number to hexadecimal, first you take the number and divide it by 16:

```
125 / 16 = 7 remainder 13
```

So we know the first digit is a 7. Now we just need to work out the second digit. We can do this by looking at the remainder, 13, which is D in hexadecimal.

$$125_{10} = 7D_{16}$$

5.2 Networks

Think-IT

5.2.4 Convert the following decimal numbers to hexadecimal and find out which manufacturers these parts of MAC addresses represent.

a) 136:117:86   **d)** 148:99:209

b) 140:86:197   **e)** 00:18:90

c) 144:73:250

Think-IT

5.2.6 Convert the following binary numbers to hexadecimal:

a) 10100001

b) 00100010

c) 10001010

d) 00011111

e) 00000111

Think-IT

5.2.5 Convert the following hexadecimal numbers to decimal:

a) IE   **c)** C6   **e)** FC

b) EA   **d)** 90

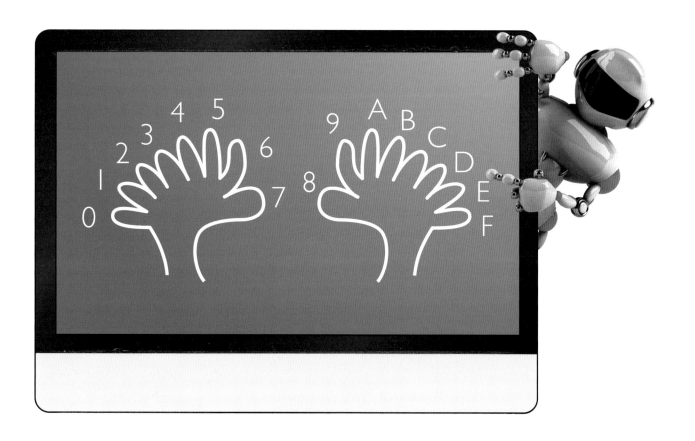

Network topologies

The topology of a network describes the layout of the devices that are connected to a LAN. The topology shows how data flows within a network, regardless of its physical design. Distances, types of physical connection and data transfer rates are not considered when looking at network topologies.

The three main network topologies are:

The bus topology

All devices on a bus topology share a single backbone cable (the bus). All messages are sent along this cable but only the intended recipient accepts and processes the data. A terminator is required at each end of the bus to stop signals going back down the line.

It is an easy network to set up and install, but if the main bus cable fails the whole network goes down. Data collisions are also very common and the security of this network is low because all the connected devices get to see the data travelling over the network.

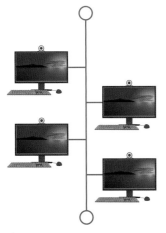

▲ The bus topology

The star topology

A star topology has a hub or a switch at the centre of the network. If there is a switch at the centre of the network, the computers in the network send their data packets to the switch and the switch makes sure it gets passed on to the correct destination. If there is a hub is at the centre, the hub receives each data packet and sends it to all the computers on the network in a scatter-gun approach. With a switched star network there is excellent security for the data because it is transmitted directly to its destination.

A star topology is more reliable than a bus topology because the network will continue to work if the cable to one device fails, as long as the hub or switch doesn't fail. It also does not suffer from data collisions. However, it is costly to install because of the amount of cable and hardware required and it is more difficult to set up than a bus topology.

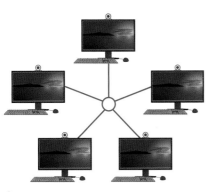

▲ The star topology

The ring topology

In a ring topology each device on the network is connected to another two devices to form a circle. The data travels in one direction around the circle. The destination for the data is identified by a token added to the data. As the data passes a node it inspects the token to see if the data is intended for that node, if yes the data is opened, if not they do not look at the data. As with a bus network the data passes through each station on the network until the destination is found so those stations between the sender and destination can see the data being transmitted.

Data collisions won't happen with a ring topology because all the data is travelling in the same direction. Another advantage of a ring network is the ability to determine exactly how long data will take to travel from source to destination. However, just like the bus topology, the network fails if just one cable fails, breaking the circle.

If a **wireless access point** is used as part of the network then devices will be able to connect to a wired network through the wireless access point and use Wifi to share network resources.

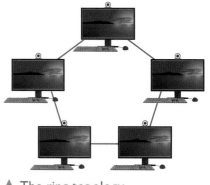

▲ The ring topology

Key term

Wireless access point: A device that allows wireless devices to connect to a wired network using Wifi.

Challenge

Do you remember the challenge for this unit, to build and test a network? Well, it's time to get on with it …

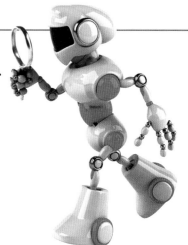

Compute-IT

5.2.7 a) Design a network for use in a small area, such as a home or a small business, and build and test that network.

b) Explain the decisions you made about the topology, the devices you included on the network and the network addressing used.

Think-IT

6.1.1 Why do Amazon, Facebook and YouTube allow you to create an account on their websites? Do all three companies have the same reason for allowing you to create an account? Are the reasons for allowing you to create an account for your benefit, as the user, or does the company also benefit?

Challenge

Your challenge for this unit is to build a web page that allows users to fill in a form to search for data within a database and to build a server-side script page that uses SQL to look for the data and return the results to the screen.

6.1 Web forms and client-side scripting

Sign-up forms

Many websites, even sites you do not pay to use, require you to sign up and log in to use them. This is so the website can tailor its services specifically to your needs and browsing habits, giving you a more personal experience and providing you with targeted adverts. The majority of web sign-up forms are comprised of similar elements.

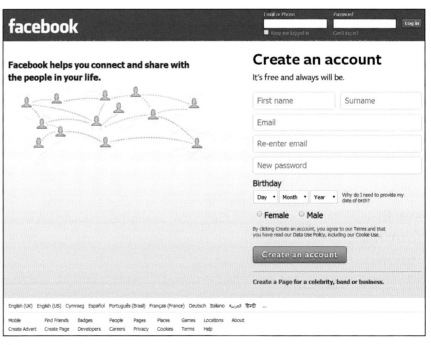

▲ Facebook's sign-up page

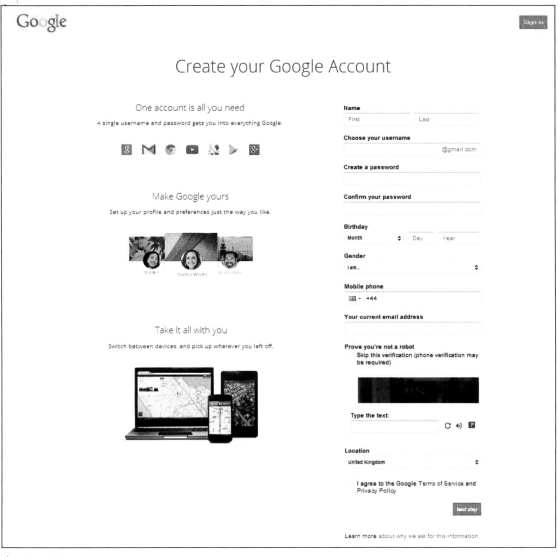

▲ Google's sign-up page

Think-IT

6.1.2 Look at the Facebook and Google sign-up screens. Make a list of the similar components you can see.

HTML forms

Web forms are created using HTML tags. All of the elements of a form are enclosed within a `<form>` tag.

```
<form>
     Form elements go here
</form>
```

The form tag is made up of a number of different attributes, listed in the table on the next page.

Plan-IT

6.1.3 Using a wireframe, plan a sign-up page for a website for a band call 'Drawn Down'. Think about the layout of the form and consider the details you will need from the user to create their profile.

Attribute	Value (the data or data type in the attribute)	Description
`name`	text	The name of the form.
`id`	text	The id that is used to identify the form in scripting.
`method`	post	'post' adds form data to the body of the HTTP request.
	get	'get' adds form data to the URL.
`action`	url	The web page where the data entered onto the form will be sent when it is submitted.
`onsubmit`	Javascript function	We can call on a Javascript function to check that the data we have entered is in the correct format before the form is submitted.

This is a simplified form tag used on the Facebook sign-up page:

```
<form method="post" id="reg" name="reg"
action="https://m.facebook.com/r.php" >
```

> The name and id of this form is `reg`. When it is submitted, it posts the data it contains to the `r.php` page on the `m.facebook.com` server in the `facebook.com` domain.

The elements of the form supply the content that allows the user to enter the required details. There are a number of different form elements that can be used.

`<input>` and `<label>`

`<input>` creates an input box for the user to type into, a button for the user to select or a button for the user to submit the form.

The attributes of the `<input>` element of a form are:

Attribute	Value	Description
`type`	text	The type of input box on the form. This is just a selection of the types of input box available.
	password	
	radio	
	checkbox	
	submit	
`name`	text	The name of the input box.
`id`	text	The id of the input box, which is used to link it to the label for the submit button.
`value`	text	The default value of the input box.
`tabindex`	number	The order in which the input boxes are accessed by pressing the tab key.

`<label>` creates a label for the `<input>` box.

The attributes of the `<label>` element of a form are:

Attribute	Value	Description
for	text	The name of the input box that the label belongs to.

For example:

`<label for="userName">Username</label>` `<input id="userName" name="userName" type="text">`	Username [ ]

`<label for="password">Password</label>`
`<input id="password" name="password"`
`type="password">`
	Password [.............]

`<label for="sex">Male</label>`
`<input id="sex" name="sex" type="radio" value="Male">`
`<label for="sex">Female</label>`
`<input id="sex" name="sex" type="radio" value="Female">`
	Male ◯
	
	Female ◯

`<label for="transport">Bus</label>`
`<input id="transport" name="transport"`
`type="checkbox" value="bus">`
`<label for="transport">Car</label>`
`<input id="transport" name="transport"`
`type="checkbox" value="car">`
	Bus ☐
	
	Car ☐

`<input id="submit" name="submit" type="submit"` `value="Submit Form">`	Submit Form

The `<select>` and `<option>` tags

The `<select>` and `<option>` tags are used to create a dropdown list for the user to select items from. All of the `<option>` tags, which create an option in the dropdown list, must be within a parent `<select>` tag:

`<select>`

`<option>`

`<option>`

`</select>`

The attributes of the `<select>` tag are:

Attribute	Value	Description
name	text	The name of the dropdown list.
id	text	The id of the dropdown list is used to link it to its label.

The attributes of the `<option>` tag are:

Attribute	Value	Description
value	text	The value of the option if selected.

For example:

```
<select id="keyStage" name="keyStage">
    <option value="ks1">KS1</option>
    <option value="ks2">KS2</option>
    <option value="ks3">KS3</option>
    <option value="ks4">KS4</option>
</select>
```

Compute-IT

6.1.4 Program the website sign-up page you designed for 6.1.3 Plan-IT. Leave the action attribute in the `<form>` tag blank for now as you do not yet have a page to receive the data. Make sure your form contains a submit button so the user can send their data and don't forget to include the HTML basics (`<html>`, `<head>` and `<body>`).

Form validation with client-side scripting

It is vital that a web page receives the correct type of data because incorrect data is of no use or may result in unintended consequences. A process called **data validation** is used to check that the data a user enters is sensible and usable and, if it isn't, to tell the user that they have made a mistake.

Most data validation on web pages is carried out on the user's computer before the data is submitted to the server. Code that runs on a user's computer is called a **client-side script**. The most popular programming language for client-side scripting is **Javascript**.

Javascript is often written within a `<script>` tag in the `<head>` section of the web page although it can be written just before the closing HTML tag, `</html>`, or included as an external file. It is often activated by an event that is generated when the user does something on a web page, like clicking on a button or submitting a form.

Key terms

Data validation: The process of checking that data entered is sensible and usable.

Client-side script: Website code that is run on the user's computer rather than on the server.

Javascript: A programming language that is often used to write client-side scripts for websites.

There are a number of HTML events that can be used as attributes in HTML tags. Here are some of the most popular ones:

Attribute	Description
onload	The event occurs once the HTML page has been loaded. The attribute is used in the `<body>` tag.
onsubmit	The event occurs when the user submits the form. The attribute is usually placed in the `<form>` tag.
onkeypress	The event occurs when the user presses a key on the keyboard.
onclick	The event occurs when the user clicks on the web page element.
ondblclick	The event occurs when the user double clicks on the web page element.
onmouseover	The event occurs when the user places their mouse cursor over the web page element.

Here is a simple HTML page with a button on it. The `onclick` event calls a Javascript function called `messageBox()`. This function simply calls the built-in alert function that makes an alert box appear with the given text.

```
<html>

<head>

<script type="text/Javascript">

    function messageBox(){

        alert("Whoohoo!");

    }

</script>

</head>

<body>

    <input type="button" value="Click me!"
    onclick="messageBox();" >

</body>

</html>
```

> **Curly brackets are used to show where the function begins and ends.**

> **Single lines of Javascript code always end with a semi-colon. JavaScript is case sensitive too.**

Compute-IT

6.1.5 Write a Javascript function for the sign-up page you programmed for 6.1.4 Compute-IT. It should display an alert to the user when the form is submitted using the `onsubmit` event.

Validating data on a web form

Using Javascript and event handling, it is possible to validate web forms before we submit them. We can define a validating function that returns a Boolean value after checking the form data. When an event occurs, we can call the function, for example `return functionName()`. The page will not be submitted if `functionName` returns `false`. The most common event to run the validation on is the `onsubmit` event in the `<form>` tag.

We can check that the user has filled in a required box and not left it empty or we can check that they have entered a valid email address. For example, this is an email Javascript validation function:

```
function validateEmail(){
    var x = document.forms["myForm"]["email"].value;
    var atpos = x.indexOf("@");
    var dotpos = x.lastIndexOf(".");
    if (atpos<1 || dotpos < atpos + 2 || dotpos +
    2 >= x.length){
        alert("Not a valid email address");
        return false;
    }
    else {
        return true;
    }
}
```

Find the position of the @ sign.

Find the position of the last full stop.

|| is the OR operator in Javascript.

This stops the page submitting.

And here is an example of an HTML form that calls the function on the `onsubmit` event:

```
<form id="mainForm" name="mainForm" method="post"
  action="receiveData.php" onsubmit="return
  validateEmail();">
```

Think-IT

6.1.6 Look at the Javascript function `validateEmail()`, which checks to see if the user has entered a valid email address. Produce a flowchart to represent this algorithm.

Plan-IT

6.1.7 Look at the sign-up page you programmed for 6.1.4 Compute-IT and decide how you could validate the data you are asking the user to provide, once they click 'Submit' and before the data can be submitted to the server. Present your ideas in a table like this:

Element type	Element ID	Validation
text	username	Check that it is not empty.
text	email	Check that it is a valid email address.

Compute-IT

6.1.8 Program the client-side scripting to validate your sign-up form, which you planned for 6.1.7 Plan-IT.

Compute-IT

6.1.9 Test and debug the program you wrote for 6.1.8 Compute-IT. Record your testing in a test table.

Test	Expected outcome	Actual outcome	Result	Screenshot
No surname entered	Alert box appears and user to click OK and enter a surname	Alert box appeared and user to click OK and enter a surname	PASS	Surname [ ] [Submit Form] JavaScript Alert ⊗ Surname cannot be empty [OK]

▲ An example of a test table

6.2 Web servers and server-side scripting

Web servers

A web server is a computer that allows web content to be accessed through the internet. Web servers require software to make this to happen, an IP address and, usually, a domain name like **www.google.co.uk**. Between them Google and Microsoft currently have over one million web servers to provide all the services they offer.

▲ One of Google's many server rooms

Plan-IT

6.2.1 Find three web-hosting companies that allow you to host a MySQL database and run PHP, a server-side scripting language. Choose which company you would use and explain your decision.

When you have built a website it is common to pay a company to host it for you. You upload the web pages to one of the web-hosting companies' web servers so the website can be publically accessed on the internet, and they offer you support and make sure your website is always active by backing up the data in case something goes wrong.

While you are developing a website you do not want the public accessing it and seeing the unfinished product, so it is usual to work on your local machine and only upload finished or updated pages to the web server.

If you are developing your site using HTML and client-side scripting it is easy to run it on your computer with no extra software, but when you need services like a database or wish to run server-side scripting languages like PHP or ASP then you need to have additional software to use your computer as a web server. A local web server is not accessible to others via the internet. The web pages on a local server can only be seen on the local computer running the software, and the url to access the website being developed when the software is running is `localhost`.

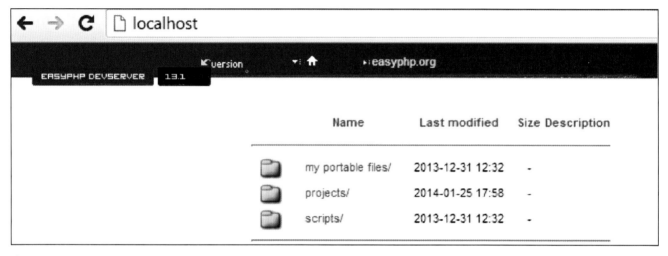

▲ A localhost web server being accessed in a web browser

WampServer and EasyPHP, which are both open source and therefore free to use, are the most popular software used to make a computer act as a web server. XAMPP, which is also open source, can be used to run a web server from software and web pages hosted on a USB stick.

Server-side scripting

Server-side script runs on a web server and processes the content of the web page that will be delivered to the client machine. This means that when the client's machine requests a web page, the server-side code that is contained within the HTML page is processed first, before the server responds to the client.

If a web page contains server-side scripting, data submitted to a web server is always evaluated before being submitted to a database. The content of the HTML sent back to the client can also be customised to meet the client's needs so not everyone who looks at the web page receives the same information.

Compute-IT

6.2.2 Set up a local web server on your computer or a USB memory stick. Test that it works by going to the localhost url in a web browser.

Key term

Server-side script: Website code that runs on a web server and processes the content of the web page that will be delivered to the client machine.

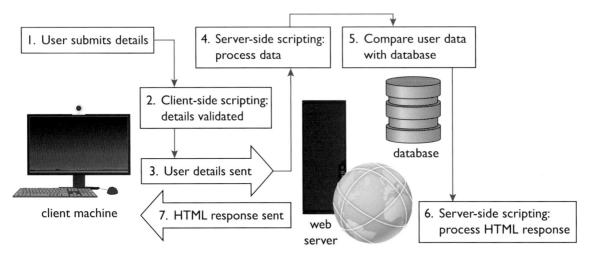

How data moves between a web client and a web server running server-side scripting. Communication between a web client and a web server is carried out according to HTTP, the hypertext transfer protocol.

Web pages that contain server-side scripting do not use the typical *.html extension. Instead they use an extension that tells the web server which language is being used. These are the most common server-side languages:

Language	Extension
ASP	*.asp
Java	*.jsp
Perl	*.cgi
PHP	*.php
Python	*.py

PHP server-side scripting

The basics

PHP script can be written anywhere within your HTML code. To open a section of PHP you use <?php and when you have finished your scripting you close it with ?>. Just like Javascript, single lines of PHP code end with a semi-colon (;).

For example, this simple piece of PHP code would output the words 'Hello World' to the web page. Running this code is a good way of testing if your web server is up and running.

```
<html>
<body>
<?php
    echo "Hello World";
?>
</body>
</html>
```

Compute-IT

6.2.3 Output your name to a web page using the echo function in PHP, to test that your web server is up and running.

To join strings together in PHP we use a dot: `.`, so

```
echo "Hello"." "."World";
```

produces the same output as the code on page 90.

   PHP is case sensitive, so the function `echo` is not the same as `Echo`. We can also include HTML tags with PHP code to format the output. For example:

```
echo "Hello<br/>World";
```

produces the output opposite:

```
Hello
World
```

Variable declarations

You do not have to define the data type of a variable. All variables are declared using a $ before their name. The names of variables cannot start with a number and must not include spaces.

Think-IT

6.2.4 Look at this code:

```
$name = "Simon";

$x = 22;

$y = 10;

$z = $x + $y;
```

What would be printed to the screen if the variable `$z` was output?

Compute-IT

6.2.5 **a)** Define two variables, '$num1' and '$num2'.

b) Set the two variables to two different numbers.

c) Multiply the variables together and store them in a third variable, '$result'.

d) Output the result to the screen.

Defining functions

In PHP, functions follow the same syntax as Javascipt. They are defined using the word `function`, followed by the name of the function you wish to create and two brackets. The function is opened and closed with a curly bracket.

Think-IT

6.2.6 Look at this code:

```
function addTwoNumbers($x, $y){
    return $x + $y;
}
```

What would the function `addTwoNumbers` return if `$x = 17` and `$y = 32`?

Compute-IT

6.2.7 **a)** Create a function called `multiplyTwoNumbers`. The function should accept two variables.

b) Multiply the variables together and return the result.

c) Call the function and output the result to the screen to check that it works.

Selection statements

Selection statements follow a similar structure to functions. They start with an 'if', an 'elseif' or an 'else', followed – if it is an 'if' or an 'elseif' – by brackets with the condition inside. A curly bracket is used to open and close the statement.

PHP has the following comparison operators:

Comparison operator	Meaning
<	less than
>	greater than
<=	less than or equal to
>=	greater than or equal to
==	equal to
!=	not equal to

PHP has the following logical operators:

Logical operator	Meaning
&&	AND operator: true if both operands are true
||	OR operator: true if at least one operand is true

Note: '||' in the table above is ASCII character 124. On the mac keyboard, this is 'shift' and '\' on the far right next to the return key.

Think-IT

6.2.8 Look at this code:

```
if ($x > $y){
    echo "X is bigger than Y";
} elseif ($x < $y){
    echo "Y is bigger than X";
} else{
    echo "X and Y are the same value";
}
```

What would be output if $x = 15 and $y = 16?

Loops

There are two types of loop available in PHP. A 'while' loop checks the condition prior to executing the code within the loop, and the 'do…while' loop executes the code once and then checks to see if it should continue looping.

Think-IT

6.2.9 Look at this code:

```
$x = 0;
$y = 10;
while ($x <= $y){
        echo $x;
        $x++;
}
```

What would be output to the screen if this 'while' loop was run?

Hint: In PHP we use ++ to mean increment the value of the variable so $x++ adds one to the variable $x.

Think-IT

6.2.10 Look at this code:

```
$x = 0;
$y = 10;
do{
    echo $x;
} while ($x < y);
```

What is the problem with the code in this 'do…while' loop?

Compute-IT

6.2.11 Create a function called `repeatString`. The function should accept two variables, one string and one integer. The integer should pass to the function and the function should loop as many times as the integer value. Each time the function loops, the string variable should be output.

Retrieving data that has been submitted to a web page using a form

When web forms are submitted, the data they contain is sent to the web server and can be retrieved using server-side scripting. For example:

```
$userName = $_POST["userName"]
```

This is the name of the HTML element you wish to retrieve.

retrieves the data submitted from an HTML web form element with the id attribute `userName` and stores it in a PHP variable called $userName.

Compute-IT

6.2.12 Create a web page to receive the data submitted from the HTML web form you have already created. Store the data in server-side scripting variables and output the data to the screen.

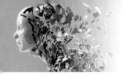

Plan-IT

6.3.1 Plan a database to hold all the data users submit when they complete the web form you have already created. Make sure you identify a primary key and use sensible field names.

6.3 Web server databases

Web server databases

Web servers often use databases to store the information necessary to produce web pages.

Connecting your database and your web page

Before you can use your database on your web page, you need to create a connection between the database you are going to build and the web page that contains your web form. PHP Data Objects, known as PDO, are a good way of creating a connection to a database.

You begin by setting out the constants you will use at the top of your web page, before the `<html>` tag. The username and password for the database, its location and the name of the database are all essential. For example:

```
$username = "admin";
$password = "4dm1n1str4t0r";
$host = "localhost";
$dbname = "schoolDB";
```

You should also state what character set you plan to use. UTF-8 is a good option because it represents all the characters in the Unicode character set, which is larger than the standard ASCII set. This allows you to store characters that do not appear in the Roman alphabet, including '¢' and '€'.

```
$options = array(PDO::MYSQL_ATTR_INIT_COMMAND =>
  "SET NAMES utf8");
```

Once you have set out the constants you will use, you can connect to the database by passing them as the values to be used to create a PDO called `$db`:

```
$db = new PDO("mysql:host={$host};dbname={$dbname};
  charset=utf8", $username, $password, $options);
```

You can begin to build your database by starting a session with this function:

```
session_start();
```

Compute-IT

6.3.2 Create a connection between the database you are going to build and the web page that receives the data once your form has been submitted.

Programming your database using PHP server-side scripting and SQL

Once you have made a connection between the database you are going to build and your web page, you can program your database using PHP server-side scripting and SQL. SQL is a structured query language used to interrogate a database and PHP server-side scripting is used to issue SQL commands to create database tables.

Creating tables

A database will have at least one table of data. A table is a collection of related data, such as the data about a country.

For example:

```
CREATE TABLE table_name
(
field1 data_type(size),
field2 data_type(size),
field3 data_type(size),
…
);
$sql = "CREATE TABLE countries
        (
        countryID int,
        countryName varchar(25),
        population int,
        continent varchar(25)
        );"
```

> **We define the SQL command to create a table and in PHP store it in a variable called $sql.**

> **The SQL statement creates a table called 'countries' with four fields: 'countryID', 'countryName', 'population' and 'continent'. The data type for each field is given after the field name and the maximum number of characters for the field is also set where appropriate, as per the PHP code that created the table.**

We then use the database connection we created to prepare the SQL for execution in a PHP script.

```
$stmt = $db->prepare($sql);
$stmt->execute();
```

The main MySQL data types are:

Data type	Description
varchar(size)	A variable length string containing letters, numbers and special characters
int	An integer
float	A number with a decimal point
date	A date in the following format: YYYY-MM-DD
datetime	A date and a time in the following format: YYYY-MM-DD HH:MM:SS

Compute-IT

6.3.3 Create a table
to store the data
submitted to your
web server using
PHP server-side
scripting and SQL.

Compute-IT

6.3.4 Insert the submitted
data from your
HTML form into
the table you have
created.

Inserting data

Once the web server receives submitted data from the web client, it can store that data in the database table using an INSERT INTO SQL statement.

The submitted data is gathered into server-side variables and then the variables are added to the SQL to be inserted into the table. This code is then executed in the same way as the SQL that created the table.

```
INSERT INTO table_name(field1, field2, field3,…)
VALUES (value1, value2, value3,…);

$countryName = $_POST["countryName"];

$population = $_POST["population"];

$continent = $_POST["continent"];
```

Retrieve the submitted data.

```
$sql = "INSERT INTO countries(countryName,
population, continent)

VALUES (:countryName, :population, :continent);

$query_params = array(":countryName" =>
$countryName, ":population" => $population,
":continent" => $continent);

$stmt = $db->prepare($sql);

$stmt->execute($query_params);
```

Prepare the data in an array and pass it into the SQL.

Retrieving data

Once the data is stored in the database we need some way of retrieving this data. Typically there will be a new web page linked to the database that is able to search for and retrieve specific data.

To retrieve records from the database, we need to use a SELECT statement.

```
SELECT field1, field2,…
FROM table_name;

$sql = "SELECT countryName, population, continent
FROM countries";
```

returns **all** the records from the table.

We do not always want to return all the records however. Sometimes we just want to check if a particular record exists. For this we need to add an extra line to our SQL, a 'WHERE' condition.

The following SQL will just return the record whose
'countryName' field is equal to 'Japan'.

```
$sql = "SELECT countryName, population, continent
FROM countries
WHERE countryName = 'Japan'";

$stmt = $db->prepare($sql);
$stmt->execute();

$row = $stmt->fetch();
```

We execute the SQL in the same way, but this time we also fetch the records and hold them in the variable $row.

If a single record has been returned, we can simply output
the data by using the echo function:

```
echo $row['countryName']." ".$row['population'].
" ".$row['continent'];
```

This would output the following data to the page: Japan 127341000 Asia

However, sometimes more than one record is returned and
we want to output them all to the screen. To do that we
need to use a loop like this:

```
for($i=0; $row = $sql->fetch(); $i++){

    print $row['countryName']." ".
    $row['population']." ".$row['continent']."<br/>"

}
```

Challenge

Do you remember the challenge at the start of the
unit, to build a web page that allows users to fill in
a form to search for data within a database and to
build a server-side script page that uses SQL to
look for the data and return the results to the
screen? You have already created a database by
linking a web page to it to insert data. Using what
you have learned, complete the challenge.

Compute-IT

6.3.5 Build a web page that allows users to fill in a
form to search for data within your database,
and create a server-side script page that uses
SQL to look for the data and returns the
result(s) to the screen.

Unit 7 Digital circuits

Challenge

Your challenge is to build a digital security alarm.

7.1 Switches and gates

Switched on

You use electrical **switches** many times every day. Some of these switches will be mechanical devices that operate by making or breaking a circuit. What you may not realise is that electrical switches also enable computers to process data.

From your science lessons you will be familiar with electrical circuits and will know that switches can either be open or closed. In fact a number of different terms are used to describe whether or not a switch is on or off. These are summarised in the table below.

Switch ON	Switch OFF
closed	open
l	0
high	low
true	false

One way of thinking about a switch is as a human interface with an electrical circuit. It is the way we input our wish for a circuit to be on or off.

When two or more switches are combined together they can be used to carry out more ingenious functions.

Bank vault access

To prevent an unscrupulous employee cleaning out a bank's vault it has been fitted with an electronic lock. The motor that opens the vault door can only be switched on if two employees simultaneously close a pair of security switches. A security switch is one that needs a key to operate it.

You can see from the circuit diagram that closing just one switch will not work. Both switches A and B must be closed to start the motor that opens the vault.

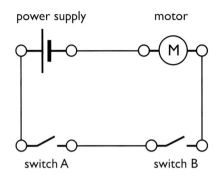

▲ A circuit diagram of a bank vault's electronic lock

Compute-IT

7.1.1   A stairway has a light over it. If someone turns on the light at the bottom of the stairs they must be able to turn it off at the top. It must also still be possible for someone else to turn the light on again at the bottom of the stairs.

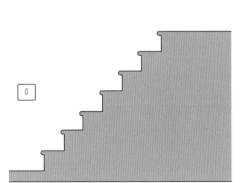

a) Using the following components, model the stairway light circuit:

- 3V power supply
- lamp (to match a 3V power supply)
- two single pole double throw switches (SPDT)
- connecting leads.

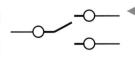

◀ The circuit symbol for a single pole double throw (SPDT) switch. An SPDT switch has a single contact or pole that can be switched between two other contacts. This gives it the name double throw. It can switch the circuit on or off in either position.

b) Draw a circuit diagram to illustrate the working stairway light.

Compute-IT

7.1.2   An electric motor is connected to a washing line to wind out the washing to dry. When the washing is dry the motor winds it back in again. The motor control switch must therefore have three positions, forward, reverse and off. This is a job for a double pole double throw (DPDT) switch.

▲ A motorised washing line

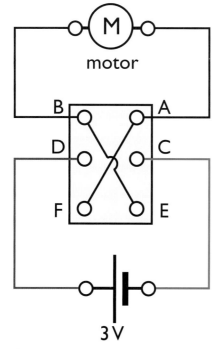

▲ A DPDT switch wiring diagram and a photograph of a DPDT switch

The DPDT switch has six contacts, which have been labelled A to F in the wiring diagram. D is always positive and C is always negative. When B is positive the motor turns clockwise. When B is negative the motor turns anticlockwise.

a) When the switch is in the top position, D connects to B and C connects to A.
   i) Will B be positive or negative?
   ii) Will the motor turn clockwise or anticlockwise?

b) When the switch is in the bottom position, D connects to F and C connects to E.
   i) Will B and E be positive or negative?
   ii) Will the motor turn clockwise or anticlockwise?

Logic gates

Digital logic is the foundation for digital computers. If you want to understand the architecture of computers you need to know about digital logic and digital circuits.

As we saw from the bank vault example, electrical circuits can act as 'gate keepers'. To open the bank vault, security switch A AND security switch B must both be closed at the same time. We can make use of electrical circuits in this way because their operation is predictable, reliable and logical. Systems that are predictable, reliable and logical are known as **logic gates**.

Logic gates perform basic logical functions. They are the fundamental building blocks of all digital circuits, including those that make up modern computers. Logic gates follow the rules of Boolean logic: the inputs are binary (0s or 1s) and the inputs determine the output, which is also a binary value.

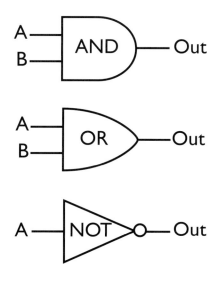

▲ The symbols used to represent the AND, OR and NOT logic gates in circuit diagrams

Digital circuits consist of one or more electrical logic gates. Digital circuits are sometimes known as Boolean circuits because they perform logical operations.

The various inputs and resulting outputs for a particular logic gate can be recorded in a table known as a truth table. In the examples in 7.1.3 Compute-IT on the next page, two switches, A and B provide the inputs and the lamp is the output. An open switch is represented by '0' and a closed switch is represented by '1'. If the lamp is on, the output is recorded as '1' and if it is off it is recorded as '0'.

> **Key term**
>
> **Digital logic**: A branch of logic that follows the rules of Boolean algebra.
>
> **Logic gates**: Simple electronic representations of Boolean logic functions. They are the fundamental building blocks of digital integrated circuits.

> **Key term**
>
> **Digital circuits**: Electrical circuits that rely on logic gates for their operation.

Think-IT

7.1.3   Copy the truth tables for the AND gate and the OR gate. Then, using the circuit diagrams to help you, complete the 'Out' column to indicate whether the lamp output will be 'I' or '0'.

a) AND gate

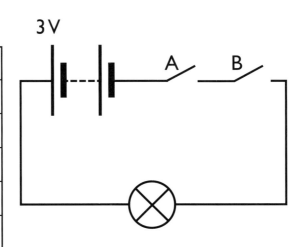

AND gate		
A	B	Out
0	0	
0	I	
I	0	
I	I	

b) OR gate

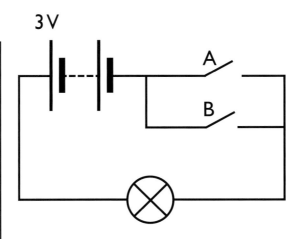

OR gate		
A	B	Out
0	0	
0	I	
I	0	
I	I	

The simplest logic gate is the NOT gate or inverter. It is used in combination with other gates to invert the input. So if the input to the NOT gate is 'on' then the output will be 'off' and if the input is 'off' then the output will be 'on'.

The truth table for the NOT gate is as follows:

NOT gate	
A	Out
1	0
0	1

When a NOT gate is linked to an AND gate, the resulting NOT AND gate combination is known as a NAND gate. When a NOT gate is linked to an OR gate, the resulting combination is known as a NOR gate.

▲ The symbols used to represent the NAND and NOR logic gates in circuit diagrams. The small circle to the right of each symbol stands for the NOT gate or inverter.

Think-IT

7.1.4   Copy and complete the truth tables for the NAND and NOR gates by applying Boolean logic. Note the shorthand symbols for these gates as shown in the diagram.

2-input NAND gate			2-input NOR gate		
A	B	Out	A	B	Out
0	0		0	0	
0	1		0	1	
1	0		1	0	
1	1		1	1	

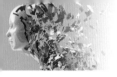

7.2 Semiconductors

From valves to transistors

Early computers, such as Colossus, made use of thousands of thermionic valves. These valves were sealed containers, usually tube shaped, made of glass and designed to perform Boolean operations. Vacuum tubes consumed a lot of power and were fragile because of the heat generated when an electric current is passed through a vacuum. Tommy Flowers identified that the glass tubes tended to break when Colossus was switched on and off, so Colossus was never switched off!

Shortly after the end of the Second World War, the solid state transistor replaced the bulkier and less reliable valve in a new, second generation of computers. Since then, **semiconductors** in the form of transistors have had an enormous impact on our society. Anything that is computerised or uses radio waves depends on **transistors**.

> ### Key terms
>
> **Semiconductor**: A device made of a semiconducting material, typically silicon, but sometimes gallium arsenide or other material.
>
> **Transistor**: A type of semiconductor used to switch electrical power. The transistor is the basic building block of all digital circuits.

▲ A small section of Colossus' circuitry, showing some of the hundreds of valves that needed to be replaced frequently

The transistor was developed in 1947 by John Bardeen, Walter Brattain and William Shockley. As the basic building block for electronic circuits, without transistors there would be no radio or television, no mobile phones or computers and no electronic equipment for control systems or medical diagnosis. Transistors are possibly the most important invention of the 20th century, and the inventors were jointly awarded the 1956 Nobel Prize in Physics for their achievement.

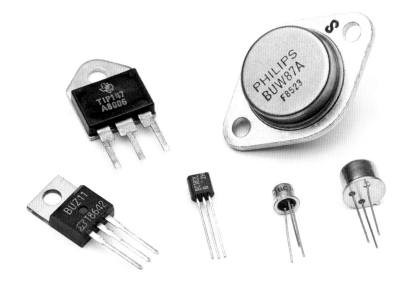

▲ Assorted transistors

A transistor is a semiconductor because it is made of a semiconducting material, typically silicon. Semiconducting material conducts electricity better than an insulator, but not as well as a conductor. Transistors have three 'legs' to connect them into a circuit. These connections are known as the collector, the base and the emitter.

The transistor acts like a switch. When it is open no current will flow through the transistor. However, if a current is applied to the base of the transistor, closing it, current will flow between the collector and the emitter.

The output from transistors has two possible states:

■ The high voltage state, when the current flows through the transistor and the output corresponds to 1. Note that the exact voltage of the output will depend on the voltage of the power supply.
■ The low or zero voltage state, when the current is too small to give an output, which therefore corresponds to 0.

Because transistors are like a 'gate' that can be opened by an electric current, logic circuits are based on the transistor.

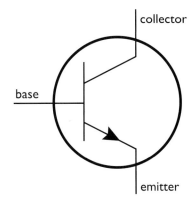

▲ A transistor circuit symbol

Warning!

Semiconductors can become very hot when operating. This is why computers need cooling fans to stop the CPU from overheating as it processes data.

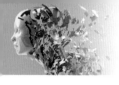

Processing data

To understand how digital circuits process data, you must first understand how a transistor can be made to function as a logic gate. We will begin by looking at the simplest gate, the NOT gate.

Study the circuit diagrams below:

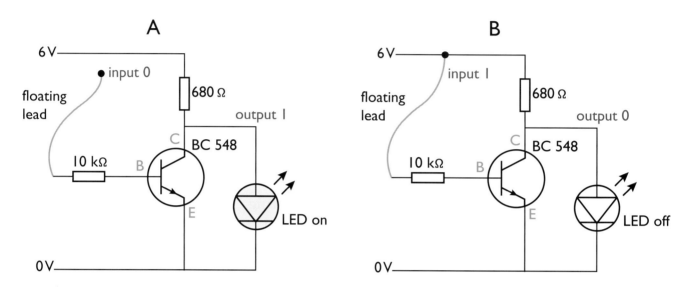

The orange floating lead provides an input. It is connected via the 10 kΩ resistor to the base of the transistor. A resistor reduces the electrical current that flows through a circuit. Resistance is measured in ohms or Ω. kΩ is kilohms or 1000 ohms.

In circuit A, the output is '1' and the LED is on. This is because the floating lead has been left floating; it is not connected. In other words, the input is low or '0' so the transistor does not conduct any current. The current flows through the LED instead.

In circuit B, the base of the transistor has been connected, via a 10 kΩ resistor, to the 6 volt power supply. The current flowing into the base of the transistor enables the current to flow through the transistor. This creates a short circuit so current no longer flows through the LED. The output is now '0' and the LED is off.

The circuit is an inverter or NOT gate.

> ### Key term
>
> **Breadboard**: A baseboard for building electrical circuits without the need for a soldering iron.

Compute-IT

7.2.1   You will gain a better understanding of digital circuits if you build and experiment with them. Study the NOT gate breadboard plan and build a NOT gate for yourself.

Begin by examining the transistor carefully. You will notice that it has three wires or 'legs'. Work out which leg is the Collector (C), which is the Base (B) and which is the Emitter (E).

On the breadboard plan, the Emitter is marked with a purple connection, the middle connection is the Base and the third connection is the Connector.

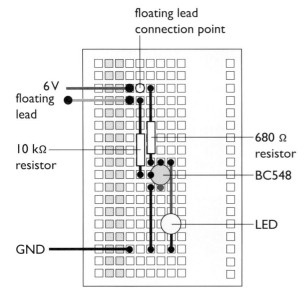

▲ A NOT gate circuit breadboard plan.
Breadboard is a baseboard for building electrical circuits without the need for a soldering iron. 'GND' means 'ground' or 'earth'

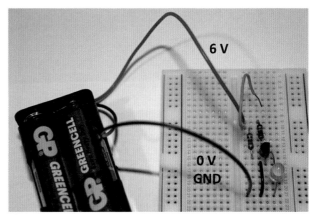

▲ A photograph of a NOT gate circuit built on breadboard

When you have completed the circuit, connect it to a 6 volt battery. To test the gate you will need to make the input high or 'I'. This is done by connecting the flying lead to the 6 V supply at the connection point. Observe the LED to see if the output is 'I' (LED on) or '0' (LED off).

Now make the input low or '0' by disconnecting the floating lead. Observe the LED to see if the output is 'I' (LED on) or '0' (LED off).

Complete the truth table for the NOT gate:

NOT gate	
A	Out
I	
0	

A —|NOT >o—Out

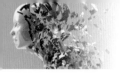

Compute-IT

7.2.2 Look at the circuit diagram and breadboard plan of a logic gate built using electronic components. If possible, build the circuit for yourself.

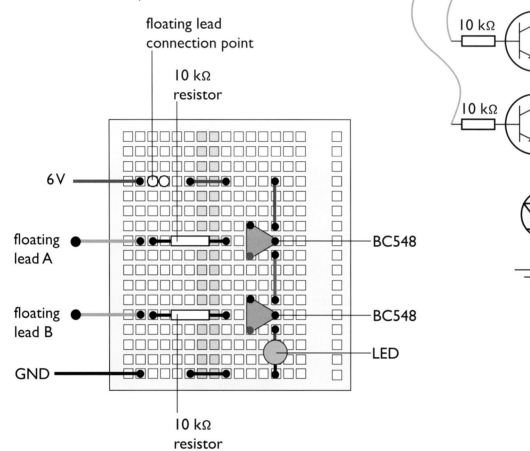

a) When just floating lead A is connected to 6 volts, will the LED be on or off?

b) When just floating lead B is connected to 6 volts, will the LED be on or off?

c) What will happen when both floating leads are connected to 6 volts?

d) What will happen if neither floating lead is connected to 6 volts?

e) What type of gate is this?

f) Create a truth table for this gate.

Compute-IT

7.2.3 Look at the circuit diagram and breadboard plan of a logic gate built using electronic components. If possible, build the circuit for yourself.

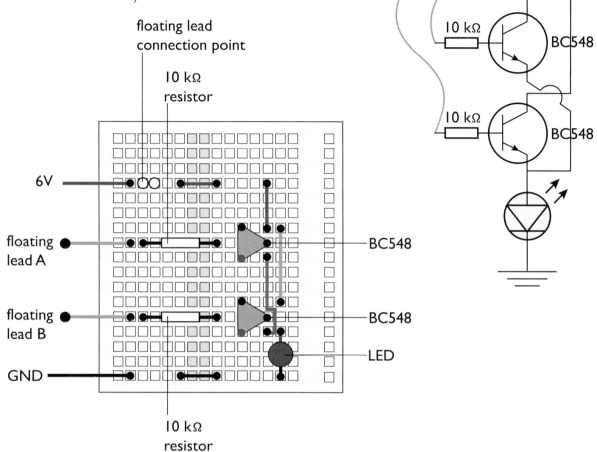

a) When just the top floating lead is connected to 6 volts, will the LED be on or off?

b) When just the bottom floating lead is connected to 6 volts, will the LED be on or off?

c) What will happen when both floating leads are connected to 6 volts?

d) What will happen if neither floating lead is connected to 6 volts?

e) What type of gate is this?

f) Create a truth table for this gate.

7.3   Integrated circuits

The arrival of the microchip

The first generation of electronic computers, such as Colossus, used valves as logic gates. The valves generated large amounts of heat and were bulky and very unreliable. They quickly burned out and constantly needed replacing.

Second generation computers were built from separate transistors rather than valves. They contained boards filled with thousands of individual transistors and magnetic memory cores.

The development of the third generation of computers hinged on the use of tiny chips of silicon that had transistors printed onto them. Initially each chip had only a small number of transistors on it. Today millions of microscopic transistors are printed on each chip. The resulting circuit is known as an **integrated circuit (IC)** or microchip. Geoffrey Drummer first came up with the idea of an integrated circuit on a single chip of silicon in 1952, but it was Jack Kilby who created the first silicon chip in 1954. Kilby's chip was improved by Robert Noyce and, together, Kilby and Noyce are regarded as the co-inventors of the microchip.

▲ One of the hundreds of valves that acted as logic gates in first generation computers

Key term

Integrated circuit (IC): A large number of digital circuits integrated together on a chip of silicon. An IC is also called a 'microchip'.

▲ A 555 integrated circuit. The 555 IC is a very simple microchip with only a handful of integrated components. It is commonly used as a timer and pulse generator, but it has many other applications. It is very cheap to purchase and when combined with a handful of additional components can be used in wide range of interesting and exciting electronics projects. It is the perfect starting point for the beginner.

Where are integrated circuits used?

Integrated circuits are found in all modern electronic devices, from washing machines to mobile phones to traffic lights to the International Space Station. The continual decrease in the size of electronic devices is possible because of the increasing miniaturisation of transistors. The development of the IC has enabled electrical engineers to pack more and more transistors into the same space. Today's ICs commonly contain millions of transistors on a silicon chip the size of a fingernail. The width of each conducting line in the circuit is measured in the tens of nanometres.

Think-IT

7.3.1 What is a nanometre? Carry out some research to find out.

The 555 IC circuit shown below is a timer circuit. The CPU needs to process instruction code in strict sequence so being able to keep time is a vital function of the processor. The circuit will make the LED pulse or flash at a regular interval when the blue button is pressed. The pulse rate can be adjusted by changing the value of the capacitor.

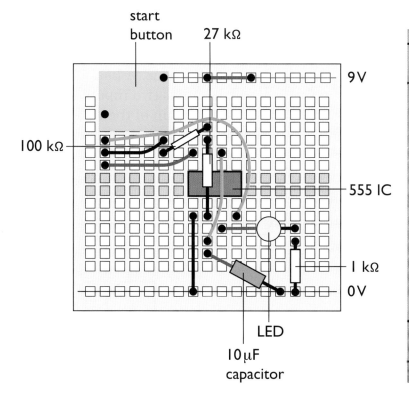

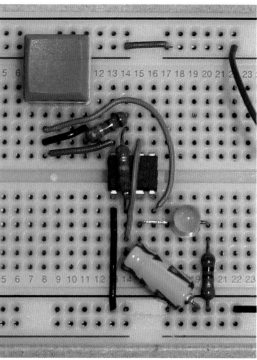

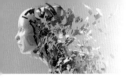

Compute-IT

7.3.2 a) Obtain an integrated circuit and examine it with a magnifying glass. You will not be able to see the microchip that is embedded inside the plastic casing. Why do you think the microchip is embedded in plastic?

b) Make a drawing of the IC, find and label the features listed below and then carry out some research to find out the function of each feature:

- the black plastic case surrounding the microchip
- the manufacturer's logo
- a part number printed on the top of the case
- rows of metal pins protruding from the case. How many pins does your IC have?
- a small dot, notch or dimple at one end of the IC case.

Doing the sums

We have seen how digital circuits can process data in the form of simple binary inputs and outputs, but how can computers follow complicated instructions in code in order to process data involving many binary inputs and how do they store data that has been processed?

In fact, all that the CPU needs to do is add binary numbers and a digital circuit known as the 'half **adder**' carries out this simple piece of arithmetic. A half adder can be built from five logic gates. It has two inputs, A and B, and two outputs, S and C. S is the sum of the two binary digits and C is the carry should the addition produce one.

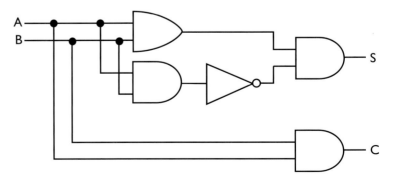

▲ A half adder logic circuit diagram

Compute-IT

7.3.3 Study the half adder logic circuit diagram.

a) List the gates that you can identify.

b) Copy and complete the truth table for the S (sum) and C (carry) outputs.

Inputs		Outputs	
A	B	C	S
0	0		
1	0		
0	1		
1	1		

Hint: Copy the half adder logic circuit diagram and write down the inputs and the resulting outputs as shown. This will help you to follow the rules of Boolean logic as you model the processing through the half adder from left to right.

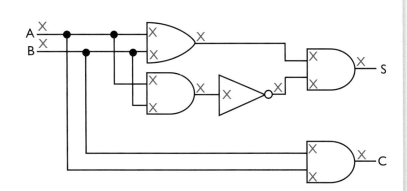

c) Check that the half adder has added the two inputs correctly by adding them yourself.

Two half adders are combined to create a full adder. The full adder has three inputs, A, B and Cin. A and B are the two bits to be added and Cin is for a carry bit from a previous calculation. The full adder has two outputs, S for the sum of the three numbers and Cout for a carry. When added together the three bits A, B and Cin will either give 0, 1, 2 (a carry out) or 3 (a sum bit and a carry out).

Once we have a basic calculating unit in the form of a digital circuit that can add two single-digit binary numbers it is just a question of scale. The CPU at the heart of a computer that carries out millions of calculations every second simply contains millions of circuits like this. The reason that computers appear to be doing something very clever and complicated is the sheer speed at which they can carry out enormous numbers of parallel processing tasks.

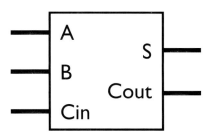

▲ A full adder circuit symbol

Compute-IT

7.3.4 Copy and complete the truth table for a full adder:

A	B	Cin	S	Cout
0	0	0		
1	0	0		
0	1	0		
0	0	1		
1	1	0		
1	0	1		
0	1	1		
1	1	1		

7.4 Can circuits remember?

Memory cells

When you carry out mental arithmetic you have to keep track of the calculation in your head. You need to remember the instructions you have been given, store numbers to be carried over and keep track of the calculation to make sure that you complete it in the correct sequence. This is very similar to the way that a computer processes data, but of course the CPU uses binary digits. Just like humans, computers need fast-acting, working memory to carry out processing tasks. Memory used during processing needs to be read from, and written to, very quickly. It is known as **main memory** and consists of enormous numbers of memory circuits known as memory cells. It is designed for rapid access by the CPU when processing.

An electronic memory cell is also known as a **latch** or a flip flop. A latch is the name given to a circuit that can exist in two stable states, high or low, and will remain in that state until it is reset.

To understand how a latch circuit can store data we will look at the simplest unit of memory, a 1-bit electronic memory cell. Each memory cell stores a single bit of data, just one binary digit, a '1' or a '0'. Once the data has been stored in the memory cell it will remain there in a stable state until it is overwritten with new data.

▶ Areas of the frontal cortex in the brain are thought to be involved in human working memory.

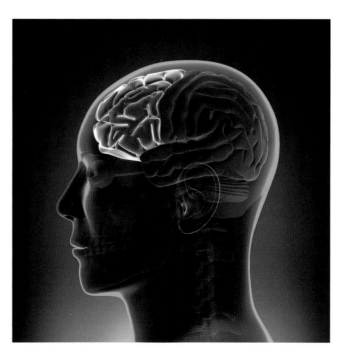

114

Think-IT

7.4.1 Study the latch circuit and notice that the two transistors are cross-linked, with the collector of T1 connected to the base of T2 and vice versa.

Let's imagine that output 'Q' is low, representing no data stored in the memory cell. Use logical reasoning to work out which of the two possible outcomes provided is correct for each step of the process.

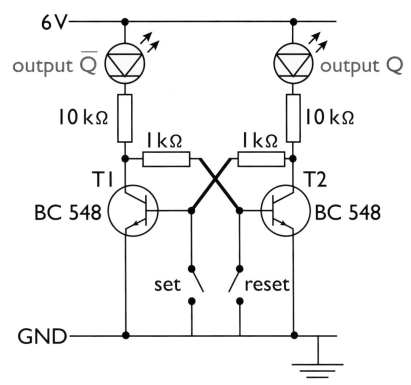

▲ A simple latch circuit.

To store a bit of data in the memory, the set switch is closed and:

- the base of T1 will become low/high
- T1 will conduct/not conduct
- output $\overline{Q}$ will be turned on/off.

The current will then flow to the base of T2 and:

- T2 will conduct/not conduct
- output Q will be turned on/off
- the current to the base of T1 will be held low/high.

The memory cell has now been set and it will remain latched in this state until the reset switch is closed.

Think-IT

7.4.2 What will happen in the circuit when the reset switch is closed?

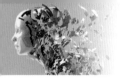

Compute-IT

7.4.3 a) Using breadboard and the components illustrated in the simple latch circuit diagram in 7.4.1 Think-IT, build and experiment with the latch circuit to find out how the memory is set and reset.

b) Once the memory is set, remove the positive lead to the battery. What happens to the data bit stored in the memory cell?

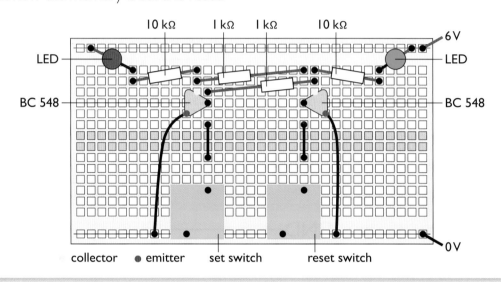

One bit is not a lot of data. You already know that it takes 8 bits to store a single byte and that one byte is needed to store a single letter. Once again it is just a question of scale. If you have enough memory cells you can store an entire application as it is running.

Moore's law

You have learned that the miniaturised transistor is the basic building block of modern computer circuits. By combining transistors together you can build logic circuits or gates that process data in the form of 1s and 0s following the rules of Boolean logic. Combinations of gates can be used to process data in different ways. They can be used to add binary digits as we saw with the half adder and to store a binary digit as we have just seen with the latch.

What makes the computer so quick and therefore so powerful is the vast numbers of transistors built into the architecture of the CPU and main memory. In 1965, Intel's co-founder, Gordon Moore, observed that the number of transistors built into the CPU doubles every two years. In 1965, computers were built from thousands of transistors. As Moore's law predicted, we now have computers built from thousands of millions of transistors.

Think-IT

7.4.4 Research Moore's law. It was developed in 1965. How accurate was it at predicting the future?

There is a minimum physical size for the transistor. Moore's law will break down when it will no longer be possible to increase the number of transistors that can fit onto a silicon chip. Although digital circuits will remain in use for many years to come, and we have not reached the limit yet, research is already being carried out that will make use of new technologies rather than the transistor to further improve performance.

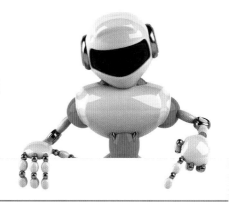

Challenge

Do you remember the challenge for this unit, to build a digital security alarm?

Compute-IT

7.4.5 Study the digital burglar alarm circuit. Once the power is on the orange LED will light up to show that the alarm is operational. The pressure pad consists of two flat copper plates, which are placed under a carpet, rug or mat. When a burglar treads on the pressure pad, the copper plates touch, the alarm is activated and the buzzer sounds. The circuit must remember that an intruder has been detected.

The circuit must latch on so that the alarm will continue to sound even if the burglar steps off the pressure pad.

a) Look at the breadboard plan below and collect all the components you will need to carry out the task.

b) Following the breadboard plan, connect the components together.

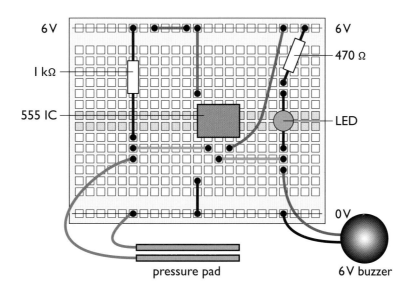

Challenge

Your challenge is to use your knowledge and research skills to compare different computer architectures.

8.1 Translators

Different languages and the need for translators

It is estimated that over 7000 languages are spoken on our planet, and that 90% of these are spoken by fewer than 100,000 people. Languages are grouped into families. For example, the Romance family of languages, which is derived from the Latin spoken by the ancient Romans, includes French, Spanish and Italian. Although languages within the same family share aspects of their vocabulary, grammar and syntax, speaking French does not mean you will automatically be able to communicate effectively in Spanish. If you were planning to carry out some important business in Spanish you might consider asking a translator to help you.

As programmers, we have a huge choice of languages we can use to write computer programs. Programming languages are also organised into families. C++ and C# are derived from C for example. And, as you already know, a program written in **source code**, in a high level programming language or assembly language, needs to be **translated** to **machine code**, the language the CPU understands.

As with natural language, knowing one programming language does not mean you will immediately be able to program in one of its related languages. However, programming languages follow stricter rules than natural languages and what you learn in one programming language translates more directly to another programming language. Programming languages share basic constructs

Key terms

Source code: The original code that a high level programming language or assembly language is written in.

Translate: In computing, 'translate' means turning program code written in a high level programming language or assembly language into machine code. There are three types of translators: assemblers, compilers and interpreters.

Machine code: The language a computer's CPU understands. Each type of CPU will have a different machine code.

and abstractions. From these, we can identify and apply general lessons from one programming language to another programming language. This generalisation is not as easy with natural languages, especially a natural language like English!

Types of translator

There are three types of translator designed to translate high level programming languages into machine code: assemblers, compilers and interpreters.

Assemblers

Assemblers convert assembly languages into object code. The object code is then output by the assembler and linked together to form machine code.

assembly language source code → object code → machine code

Compilers

Compilers take a high-level programming language, such as C, Python or Visual Basic, and translate it into object code, which is often created in the form of an executable file. The object code is then linked together to form machine code, again in the form of an executable file.

high-level language source code → object code → machine code

Interpreters

Interpreters take each line of code written in a high-level programming language such as PHP and JavaScript, one at a time, and convert it into an intermediate language. The intermediate language is often assembly language. The intermediate code is then converted into machine code. The machine code is executed.

high-level language source code → intermediate code → machine code

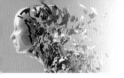

Think-IT

8.1.1 Working in pairs, decide who is going to be the programmer and who is going to be the compiler.

    a) Programmer: Create a bitmap image using a 20 × 20 grid. For example:

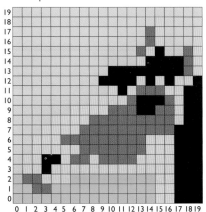

    Do not show the image to your partner. Instead, write an algorithm for the compiler containing **all** the commands they will need to recreate the image.

    b) Compiler: Follow the commands the programmer has given you.

    c) Does the image drawn by the compiler look the same as the image drawn by the programmer? Why? Why not?

    d) What are the advantages and disadvantages of translating code using a compiler?

Think-IT

8.1.2 Working in pairs, decide who is going to be the programmer and who is going to be the interpreter.

    a) Programmer: Create a bitmap image using a 20 × 20 grid. Do not show the image to your partner. Instead, write down the first command you want the interpreter to execute and pass it to your partner. Look at the result and pass the interpreter the second command. This could be a corrective command or a command to draw the next part of the image. Repeat this process until the bitmap image is complete.

    b) Interpreter: Follow the commands, showing the image you are drawing to the programmer after you have executed each command.

    c) Does the image drawn by the interpreter look the same as the image drawn by the programmer? Why? Why not?

    d) What are the advantages and disadvantages of translating code using an interpreter?

Interpreters can be more effective for use with multiple machine architectures since only the interpreter program has to be compiled for execution on each architecture. This means that the source code is inspected and translated for the machine architecture that is being used immediately, with feedback provided on any problems as each line of code is translated. In contrast, compiled programs have to be directly compiled for each architecture and re-compiled for each new architecture. Therefore, the interpreter provides machine independence by using indirection through an intermediary program that interprets and executes the code on a given machine.

A disadvantage of interpretation is that the indirection through the interpreter can lead to longer program execution times.

Using interpreted code means that the source code must be accessible, making it easier for someone else to use or adapt the code. If the source code is compiled, it is much harder to decompile it back to the original source code and therefore harder to copy or modify.

Dynamic Linked Libraries

Once a sub-program for a frequently used routine has been developed and tested, it can be placed into a library of routines that people can use within their own programs, knowing that the code has been tested and is error free. Most programming languages have Dynamic Linked Libraries of sub-programs, or routines, that can be called as required. When creating their source code, programmers will simply include a call to link to a routine. When the translator reaches this call the object code is taken from the library and run or included into the compiled object code for the program.

Integrated Development Environments

Often both compilers and interpreters are included in an Integrated Development Environment (IDE) and used at different stages of the development process. IDEs provide a range of development features including interpreters, compilers and debugging facilities to help the programmer create working programs.

Think-IT

8.1.3 Research IDEs and identify and explain the range of features they contain to help programmers.

▲ Grace Murray Hopper developed the first compiler for a programming language.

Think-IT

8.1.4 Grace Hopper is an important figure in computer science history. Research her career, identifying her contributions to computer science.

◄ Programmers can use an IDE with an interpreter and a debugger so that stop points can be placed in the code and the program can be stepped through one line at a time. Errors can be skipped or resumed. Once the errors have been ironed out, a compiler is used to create an .exe file.

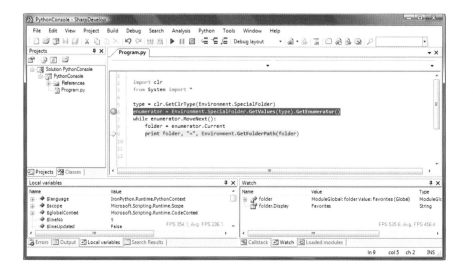

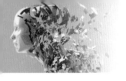

8.2 The Von Neumann and Harvard architectures

The fetch–decode–execute cycle

A **stored program computer** is a computer that stores program instructions in memory. The first stored program computer was built in England and was called the Manchester Baby.

▲ The Manchester Baby, dated 1948

The **fetch–decode–execute cycle** is an essential part of a stored program computer. It is carried out by the CPU in order to process instructions. An instruction is *fetched* from memory, *decoded* and then *executed* by the CPU. When the CPU decodes an instruction it inspects it and prepares itself to execute it. Different instructions will need to be executed in different ways.

Think-IT

8.2.1 Find an ASCII table on the internet and then fetch the next clue in the list, decode the clue by looking at the ASCII table and then execute the answer by unscrambling the letters to make a keyword.
- Find Decimal (70) in ASCII table.
- Find Hex (54) in ASCII table.
- Find Hex (48) in ASCII table.
- Find Decimal (69) in ASCII table.
- Find Decimal (67) in ASCII table.

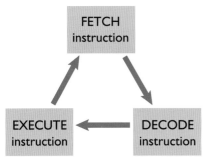

▲ The fetch–decode–execute cycle

The Little Man Computer is a model of a stored program computer that is used to illustrate the fetch–decode–execute cycle.

Imagine a little man inside a box. The man cannot see outside the box. There are two posting locations (the 'In basket' and the 'Out basket'). There are memory spaces ('Mailboxes') where instructions and data are held. There is also a program counter to point to the next instruction and a calculator for carrying out basic arithmetic.

The little man fetches the next instruction pointed to by the program counter and decodes it to find out what to do. He can collect values from the memory or from the In basket. He uses the calculator to do any calculations and can put the answer into one of the mailboxes or into the Out basket if required.

Compute-IT

8.2.2 Open a copy of the Little Man Computer at **www.cse.yorku.ca/ ~peterc/simulator/ simulator.html**. Look at the instruction set and run one of the sample programs that is provided in the tutorial.

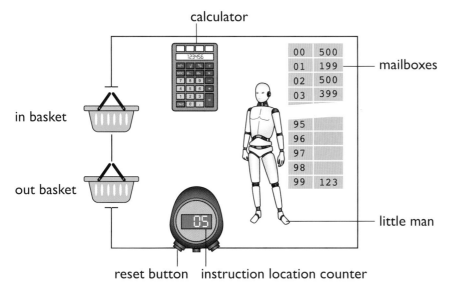

▲ The Little Man Computer model

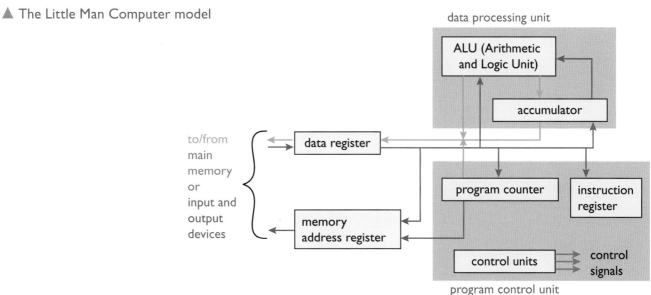

▲ The Little Man Computer model can be compared to the basic structure of a CPU.

Von Neumann architecture

The **Von Neumann architecture** consists of a number of components, including:

- memory: holds both program instructions and data
- control unit: manages the movement of program instructions and data in and out of memory, one item at a time. The control unit includes a number of registers, such as the accumulator. A register is one of a small set of data holding places that are part of a computer processor. A register may hold a computer instruction, a storage address or data
- input / output: enables the user to interact with the machine
- bus: the electrical pathway used to move data and instructions around the computer
- program counter: holds the address in memory of the next program instruction to be carried out.

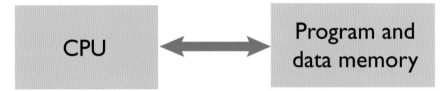

▲ The Von Neumann architecture

Two problems have been identified with the Von Neumann architecture:

- The Von Neumann bottleneck: data and program instructions both have to use the same bus, which is slow, so the CPU spends too much time waiting for instructions.
- Data and instructions occupy the same memory space. If a program is badly written, data can overwrite program instructions and vice versa.

Plan-IT

8.2.3 a) Go to **www.cse.yorku.ca/~peterc/simulator/simulator.html** and open the Little Man Computer simulator.

b) Use the following program instructions – READ, STORE, LOAD, PRINT and STOP – to write a program to get the simulator to add together two numbers that you input. Plan and then write your program using a copy of the grid below.

Line number	Instruction	Address
00		
01		
02		

Remember that data and program instructions occupy the same space so try not to overwrite data or program instructions.

c) Use the following program instructions – READ, STORE, LOAD, PRINT, STOP, SUBTRACT and BRANCHP – to write a program to get the simulator to find the larger of the two numbers that you input. Plan and then write your program, again using a copy of the grid above.

Compute-IT

8.2.4 Program and run the programs you planned for 8.2.3 Plan-IT.

Compute-IT

8.2.5 Test and debug your programs.

The Harvard architecture

The **Harvard architecture** was developed to solve the problems identified with the Von Neumann architecture. In the Harvard architecture, program instructions and data have their own dedicated bus and memory space so there are two buses and two memory spaces. Instead of program instructions and data being processed sequentially (one at a time) they are processed simultaneously (at the same time). This makes it much faster for the CPU to process. There is also no danger that program instructions will overwrite data and vice versa.

The Harvard architecture also uses pipelining. This means that data is lined up ready to be fetched so you don't have to wait for one item of data to be processed before the next item is fetched.

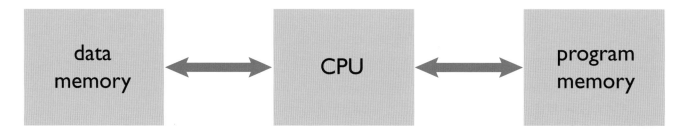

▲ The Harvard architecture

▲ ARM processors use a modified Harvard architecture and you can find them in your smart phone.

Challenge

You're now ready to complete the challenge for this unit, to use your knowledge and research skills to compare different computer architectures.

Think-IT

8.2.6 List the advantages and disadvantages of the Von Neumann architecture and the advantages and disadvantages of the Harvard architecture.

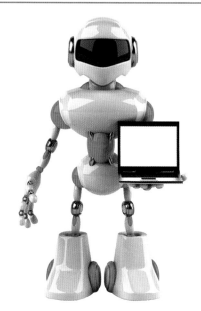

Think-IT

8.2.7 The modified Harvard architecture uses elements from both the Von Neumann architecture and the Harvard architecture. Prepare a presentation or a poster to explain the similarities and differences between the modified Harvard architecture and the Von Neumann and Harvard architectures.

◀ John von Neumann

Unit 9 Creating an app to solve a problem

Challenge

Your challenge for this unit, the last in the Compute-IT course, is to use all the knowledge, skills and experience you have developed over the last few years to create an app to solve a problem. Look around you. Is there a problem you, your fellow students, parents, teachers, teaching assistants or support staff have in, around or related to your school? Could an app help solve that problem?

9.1 An introduction to apps and app development

What is an app?

An **app** is a piece of software designed to help the user perform a specific task. It gives a digital device a sequence of instructions for completing the task, and the user interacts with the digital device through the app's user interface. There are three different types of app: web apps, native apps and hybrid apps.

Key term

App: An app, or 'application', is a piece of software designed to help the user perform a specific task. There are web apps, native apps and hybrid apps.

Web apps

Web apps are accessed through internet browsers, on desktop computers, smart phones and tablets. You do not have to visit an app store or download anything to view a web app, and it works in the same way whatever digital device you are viewing it on. Traditionally, web apps were great for simple tasks to be completed by as wide a group of people as possible because they did not make use of in-built device-specific features. But they were also slow because they were running on the web. However, the capabilities of web pages are changing rapidly as technology develops. Web apps are programmed using HTML, CSS and JavaScript.

Native apps

Native apps are built using the native programming language of the device they will be used on. This means that they can use all the in-built features a device has and are very fast, but it also means that you have to build a different version of the app for each device. For example, there is an Angry Birds app for the iPhone, one for Android phones and another that can be played on Google Chrome. This makes native apps expensive and complex to build and to maintain. When you release an update of a native app, you have to release an update for every version you support. You also have to release updates of a native app when the operating system they are designed for is upgraded, which can be very expensive!

▲ Angry Birds is a native app.

Hybrid apps

▲ What the photo? is a hybrid app.

Hybrid apps combine the flexibility across devices of web apps with the access to native functions provided by native apps. There are different ways to create hybrid apps. If you have a large budget and the quality or performance of your app is essential, then you create dedicated apps for each platform. If time and money are more limited then you can use a clever workaround. You can code in HTML, CSS and JavaScript exactly as you would if you were creating a web app, and then wrap your code in a device-specific mobile framework that gives your web app access to some of a device's native features. You can then sell your app through an app stores such as Google Play and iTunes. Hybrid apps can be slower than native apps, however, and you do have to add code to your app for each mobile framework you wrap it in. There are also a lot of mobile frameworks out there so it can be tricky trying to figure out which one to use. However, you can use one of the websites that compare different mobile frameworks to help you make your decision.

Think-IT

9.1.1 **a)** Write down the three apps that you use most frequently and then decide whether each is a web app, a native app or a hybrid app.

b) Choose a native app to explore. Which device-specific features does it use?

How do I develop an app?

We can apply computational thinking to the task of developing an app. We can decompose the task and create an algorithm that walks us through the processes we need to complete. We can also make sure that the algorithm is abstracted and generalised, so that it can be used whatever the problem the app is being designed to solve and can even be used to develop other types of products. And you will have to evaluate your work at every stage of the project.

Think-IT

9.1.2 You have come across the following terms throughout the Compute-IT course:

- **Decomposition**
- **Abstraction**
- **Generalisation**
- **Algorithm**

You have also practised the skill of **evaluation** throughout the course.

Write down a definition of each of the five concepts. Then check the glossary and, if necessary, edit your definitions to ensure that they are accurate.

App development ▶

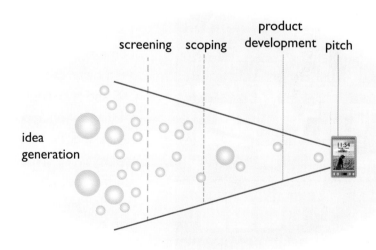

Step I: Idea generation and screening

You will begin by brainstorming lots of potential ideas, some of them big and some of them small. Then you will screen your ideas. You will evaluate them to decide which ones to put aside because they will not work, because they have been done before or because you are simply not interested in pursuing them. You will be left with one or two ideas to take forward.

Step 2: Scoping

This is the point at which you do in-depth research about those ideas that passed the screening process. You will need to establish who your target users are and what outcomes they will achieve by using your app. You will need to consider how technically difficult it might be to build an app that delivers these outcomes and where to get any data you might need to make your app work.

Step 3: Product development

Now it is time to build a simple prototype of your app and test it with your users, using their feedback to develop another iteration of your prototype.

At each stage of the process you will need to review what you have learned and decide if you need to make any changes before moving on to the next step. The app you end up with may look very different from your initial idea. This is absolutely fine! Developing an app is an iterative process.

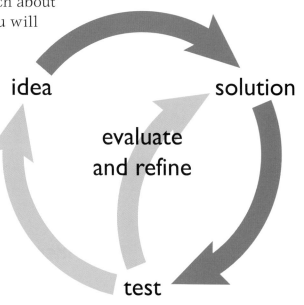

▲ Developing an app – just like developing pretty much anything – is an iterative process. Don't be afraid of change!

Plan-IT

9.1.3 You will be working in teams to develop your app, just like the people at a tech start-up company. Draw up a co-founder team agreement to set out how your team will work together. Think about the following questions:

a) How will decisions get made?

b) How will you share ownership of the finished app?

c) What will happen if one team member leaves?

d) Are there any circumstances under which a member of the team can be fired? If so, what are they? (Remember to be very specific here.)

e) Will you work outside school hours? If so, where and when?

f) How will you divide up the work? Will you each take on different roles? If so, what will they be?

9.2 Idea generation and screening

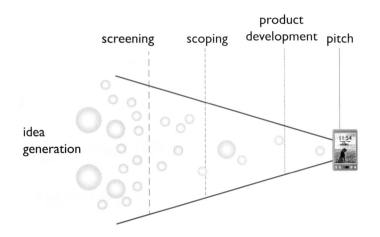

Identifying a problem

All great apps solve a problem so it's important that you fully understand the problem you are trying to solve before considering a solution. What problem are you going to solve? A brainstorming exercise is a good place to start.

Brainstorming is the name given to a collective process of idea generation, where a group of people get together and have ideas. No idea is a stupid idea. In fact, the wilder and more off-the-wall the ideas the better at this stage. And if your idea builds on an idea someone else has already had, that's great too. You're not discussing or critiquing the ideas. You're not even thinking about whether or not you can create an app to solve the problem. You are just having ideas.

> **Key term**
>
> **Brainstorming**: A collective process of idea generation.

Plan-IT

9.2.1 Hold a team brainstorming session:

a) Write this question down in the middle of a large sheet of paper: 'What problems do we have in our school?'

b) Take it in turns to write a problem onto the sheet of paper for ten minutes.

Hint: If you're having trouble coming up with a new idea, look at an idea already on the sheet of paper and ask 'Why?'

Thinking more deeply

You have identified lots of problems but you cannot build apps to solve all of them, so it is time to choose those you are most passionate about or which solve the biggest or most serious problem in your school and think about them in more detail. You need to be able to tell the story behind each problem, outlining the sequence of events that leads up to it. Only when you really understand how the problem occurs will you be able to design a solution that prevents it from happening or makes life a little easier when it does happen.

It is important that every member of your team feels strongly about the problems you choose to explore further, but sometimes it is very hard to come to any kind of agreement. When this happens, a vote can help break the deadlock. Each member of the team can put a dot against the ideas they like best and the ideas with the most votes are the ones you pursue as a team.

There are several techniques that you can use to help you tell the story behind an idea.

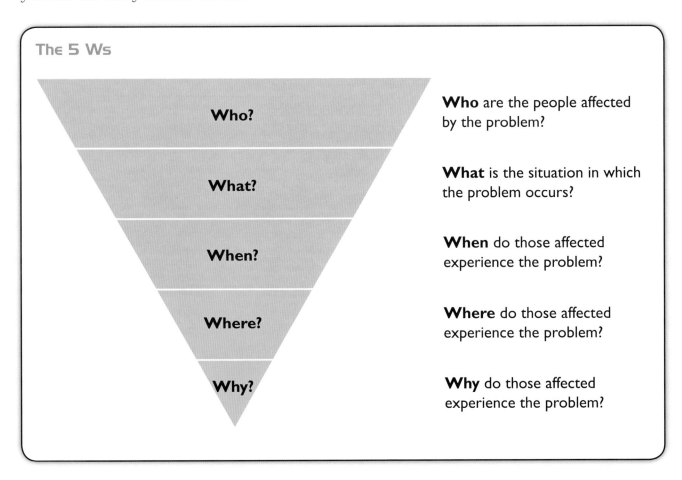

The 5 Ws

Who?

Who are the people affected by the problem?

What?

What is the situation in which the problem occurs?

When?

When do those affected experience the problem?

Where?

Where do those affected experience the problem?

Why?

Why do those affected experience the problem?

The VEX factor

Familiar
Is the problem **familiar**? Does it affect real people you can name?

Frequent
Does the problem happen **frequently** enough to justify developing a solution?

Specific
Is the problem **specific**? Can you tell the story of the problem?

Unpredictable
Is the problem **unpredictable**, so you are never quite sure when it will occur?

Expensive
Is there a **high cost** if the problem is not solved? 'Expensive' might not just mean financially expensive. There might be a high time cost or a high emotional cost attached to the problem.

Irritant
Is the problem **irritating**?

▲ Can you step into the shoes of the user to understand the problems they face?

Role play

You do not need to create a theatrical masterpiece, but stepping into the shoes of your users and acting out the difficulties they face is a great way to really understand the problem you are setting out to solve. Try to think and act like you are really affected by the problem. And keep it simple. Too many extra details will make it difficult for you to see the story behind the problem clearly.

Plan-IT

9.2.2 a) As a team choose two of the problems you identified during your brainstorming session that you would like to focus on.

b) Use either the 5 Ws or the VEX factor technique to understand each of your chosen problems in more detail.

c) Devise a short role play to tell the story behind each problem.

The elevator pitch

When you have really understood a problem you should be able to come up with an idea for an app to solve that problem. An elevator pitch can be a useful way to frame your idea.

Imagine you are in an elevator with a potential investor. It takes just 15 seconds for the elevator to rise from the first floor to the fifteenth floor. This is all the time you have to pitch your idea. To do this effectively you need to come up with a very short, clear and precise description of your idea. Your pitch should explain:

- what it is you are going to develop. Is it a web app, a mobile app or a hybrid app?
- the problem the app is going to solve
- who your target audience is. Who will benefit from the app?
- a potential feature of your app that will help solve the problem and will appeal to your target audience.

The most important thing to remember is that you will not prepare a perfect elevator pitch first time. Even though it is very short it will need to go through lots of iterations before it is right.

Compute-IT

9.2.3 Prepare an elevator pitch for each of the problems you explored in more depth for 9.2.2 Plan-IT. You can use the following structure to help you:

```
My team,
[team name],
is developing
[platform idea]
to help [target
audience] solve
a problem [with
secret sauce].
```

> **Our team, Buzzer Buddiez, is developing a mobile app to help students who have studied late and are likely to oversleep because they hit snooze on their alarm clock to wake up on time with help from friends and family.**

▲ The elevator pitch written by Buzzer Buddiez

Separating the wheat from the chaff

Once you have thought more deeply about a selection of
the problems you originally brainstormed and have drawn
up elevator pitches for your ideas, you must screen them
and separate the wheat from the chaff. You must rule out
those ideas that have obvious or significant problems and
take forward only those that you think are viable. A viable
idea is one that has the potential to succeed. You cannot
know for certain that it will succeed at this stage, but you
can look at an idea's potential for success so you spend
time and resources developing only those ideas that are
likely to succeed.

When wheat is harvested, the ▶
grain, the part of the plant that
you can eat, has to be separated
from the chaff, the dry casing
that protects the grain while it is
growing. The phrase 'separating
the wheat from the chaff'
therefore means to separate
what is valuable from what has
less value.

You can evaluate your ideas by asking a series of questions
and scoring the answers, awarding an idea 1 point if the
answer is 'yes' and 0 points if the answer is 'no'.

	Why ask the question?
Will our app be different from anything else out there?	<u>Revolutionary products</u> are usually more interesting to investors but can be very challenging to build and bring to market. <u>Evolutionary products</u> can differentiate themselves from similar products in many ways, including design, features, quality, pricing or distribution.
Will our app appeal to a target audience?	Developing products for a well-defined target audience is often easier, faster and cheaper than building a mass-market product.
Why will someone choose our app over comparable products? Does it have any stand-out features?	You should be able to point to one to three features that would benefit your users.
Will our app compete in an established market?	Establishing a new market can reap huge rewards but is difficult, time consuming and expensive. The existence of competitive products can be a sign that a market is established.
Are we really, really excited by our app idea?	Developing new products is a long and challenging process. If you are not really, really excited by an idea now, move on to the next idea.

You will need to research the market to be able to answer these questions. Try searching the internet and the app stores for similar apps. If there are not any apps out there, does the problem already have an effective non-technical solution? Non-technical solutions will also compete against your app. Remember to keep a record of your research.

The purpose of the exercise is not to identify the idea with the highest score, which automatically wins. It is to tease out whether any of your ideas have big stumbling blocks that will limit their likelihood of success and to highlight areas you will have to consider in more detail if you do decide to take your idea forward.

Do not throw away the ideas you do not take forward. Keep them on the reserve bench. You never know what might happen and it is always good to keep a couple of good ideas as back-up. The single most important quality for a tech start-up company is the ability to 'fail well'. This means that when you make a mistake or things don't go the way you would like them to for reasons beyond your control, you learn from the experience, get straight back up and try again. Remember, Angry Birds was the 52nd game created by Rovio, not its first.

Compute-IT

9.2.4 Evaluate each of your ideas and, as a group, decide which you will take forwards to the scoping phase of the process.

9.3 Scoping your idea

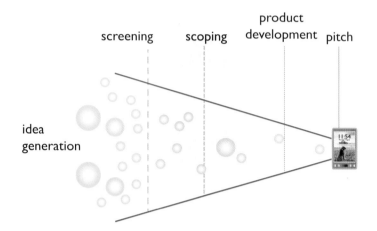

What is scoping?

The scoping phase of the development process is all about investigating in more detail the small number of ideas that made it through screening. It provides you with an opportunity to test the assumptions you have made so far and decide which app idea you are going to invest your time and energy in developing. There are three key strands to scoping:

- understanding the market
- understanding the user
- understanding the solution.

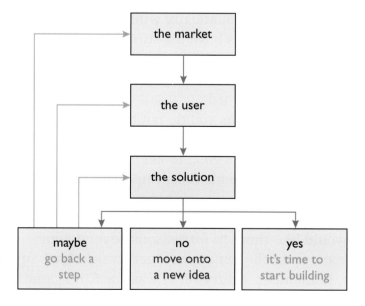

Understanding the market

Is there a solution to the problem you have identified already on the market?

Are there products out there solving similar problems? How do they work?

Who are your competitors?

Who is your target user group? How big is it?

To answer these key questions you need to dig deeper than you did during the idea generation and screening phase of the project. You need to gather data, look at it critically and really try to understand the implications of what you discover for your app.

A busy competitive environment, with other products solving the same or similar problems, shows that there are real customers out there interested in the type of product you are planning to produce, which is good news. However, if the market is more than busy, if it is crowded, then the app you are planning to develop must stand out to get noticed. If you cannot identify any competing products, then you may have struck gold and you will be the first to produce an app that customers snap up. Or you may have misjudged things and no one will be interested in your product. This phase of scoping is all about understanding the competitive environment and trying to work out where your app fits, to help you judge whether it is worth the risks involved in developing it.

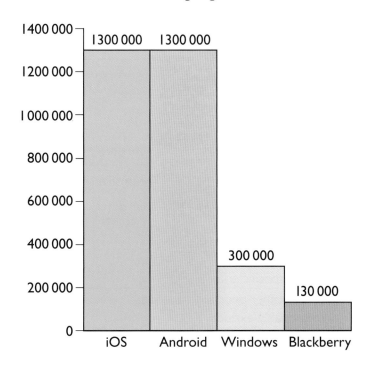

◀ There are thousands of apps out there. This graph shows the number of apps available by operating system in June 2014, but the number is growing every month. Will your app stand out from the crowd?

This phase of scoping is also about trying to work out if there are enough people who will be interested in your app to make it worthwhile developing it. If your potential market is too small then your app will sink without trace. You cannot get around this by building an app that will interest 'everyone' though. 'Everyone' invariably means 'no one', because an app that appeals to everyone is generally so generic that it does not meet the needs of any one user satisfactorily. You must identify a target user group that has a specific problem that your app is going to solve for them and that target user group has to be large enough to support your app.

Plan-IT

9.3.1 Build on the research you have already carried out to investigate your main competitors. Copy and complete the table to develop a profile for each competing product. Do not worry if you cannot complete the table. The aim of the exercise is to find out as much as you can about your competitors quickly.

Product name	
Company name	
When was the product launched? Is the product established or new to the market?	
Who is the product aimed at? Who is using it and how often? How many times has it been used or how many unique monthly visitors does it have?	
What are people saying about it online? Does it have any press reviews and user reviews? How many Twitter followers or Facebook likes does it have?	

Plan-IT

9.3.2 How big is your market size? Copy and complete the table and collect basic data about the people your product will target and then exclude those groups who are unlikely to use it. This gives you a reasonable estimate of the size of your market. Government websites are a good place to start your search.

Criterion	Number
Number of people who fit the age profile for your app	
minus people who do not have access to the appropriate technology	
minus people who do not fit any other specific criterion	
minus other people you should reasonably exclude	
Total market size	

Plan-IT

9.3.3 a) How does your idea stand up in the market?

- Is it **high risk**? Is the market crowded or are their one or two competitors that solve the problem very effectively? Is the market size very small?

- Is it **medium risk**? Are there a few competitors who solve the problem well enough but do not dominate the market? Is there plenty of scope to provide a better product?

- Is it **low risk**? Are there very few, if any, competitors but still a clear demand for a technological solution? Will the market size support your app?

b) How does your new knowledge about your competitors affect your elevator pitch, particularly your 'secret sauce'? If appropriate, produce another iteration of your elevator pitch.

Understanding the user

Once you have identified your target market, it is important to find out if there is a genuine need for your app. What are users doing at the moment to solve the problem you have identified and will they respond positively to an app-based solution? It's time to get out there, meet your target user group and find out.

Ask the right kind of questions

One of the most common mistakes made by people trying to understand their user group early on in the development of a product is to gather lots of **quantitative data** in the form of responses to closed questions. Quantitative data is very useful if you already have a product and are trying to find out your users' thoughts on specific issues to help you make decisions. It is not terribly helpful if you want to explore potential users' thoughts and feelings about a problem and need to uncover information that you do not know you need to know. In this situation it is much better to ask open questions and gather **qualitative data** from a smaller number of potential users.

> ### Key terms
>
> **Quantitative data**: data that measures things. It typically provides answers to questions like, How much market share do we have? How many customers do we have? When do people buy our product? You collect quantitative data using closed questions. You can find out more about closed questions in Unit 8 of *Compute-IT 1*.
>
> **Qualitative data**: data that focuses on understanding things. It uncovers how people think and feel about things and finds out why they behave as they do. You collect qualitative data using open questions, such as, What are the strengths of this proposal? What don't you like about our idea? You can find out more about open questions in Unit 8 of *Compute-IT 1*.

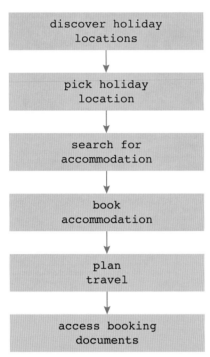

▲ An algorithm for booking a holiday

During your idea generation and screening phase you will almost certainly have thought about how the problem you want to solve comes about and it is important to check with your potential users that you are on the right track. To do this you could show them an algorithm that represents the process behind the problem, perhaps in the form of a flowchart, and ask them open questions to find out if the algorithm accurately reflects the problem as they understand it. You could also take the opportunity to find out what solutions to the problem they would like to see, before you ask them their thoughts on your proposed solution.

When you have gathered data from your target user group you must analyse it. Does it confirm what you already knew or does it teach you anything surprising? Do you need to amend your algorithm and/or your elevator pitch as a result of your findings? Remember to identify patterns in the data rather than respond to every detail.

Plan-IT

9.3.4 Create an algorithm that represents the process behind the problem your app is designed to solve.

Plan-IT

9.3.5 Prepare a questionnaire for your target user group. Include questions that:
- profile the interviewee: for example, 'What is your name?' and 'How old are you?' Remember, this is not an opportunity to be nosy, just to find out information that you know you will find useful when you are developing your app. So do not ask if they have a boyfriend or a girlfriend unless your app is all about relationships!
- find out if you have accurately and fully decomposed the problem
- find out what solutions the interviewee would like implemented to solve the problem
- find out what the interviewee thinks of your app idea. You could give them the elevator pitch you created for 9.2.3 Compute-IT and ask for their thoughts.

Plan-IT

9.3.6 Find at least five members of your target user group to complete your questionnaire.

Plan-IT

9.3.7 Analyse the data you collected and, if appropriate, produce another iteration of your algorithm and/or your elevator pitch.

Understanding the solution

To be successful, an app has to work. It has to be technically feasible and you need to be able to source all the data you need to make it work.

Keep it technically simple

Automatic image recognition, voice recognition and automatic translation, and the ability to edit large files, such as video files, on a mobile device are all emerging, expensive and unreliable technologies. As a result, it is best to avoid them when you design your app and to focus on developing a simple technical solution that addresses the problem you have set out to tackle. You should also use tools that are available to help you, such as libraries of open source code written by other developers.

This case study illustrates how it is possible to re-think your solution to fit the technological realities you have to work with.

Compute-IT

9.3.8 Is your solution technically possible? If not, are there technically simpler ways to solve this problem? Which type of app – a web app, a native app or a hybrid app – would be best for your solution?

Transit

The problem: Bengali students are often expected to translate conversations between their Bengali parents, who cannot speak English, and their teachers, who cannot speak Bengali. Sometimes students mis-translate the conversations to avoid getting into trouble.

The initial solution: An automatic speech-to-speech translation. But the feedback from experts was clear: it cannot be done. It would be very expensive to build and even if you did manage to build it, it would be very unreliable.

The re-envisioned solution: The Transit team realised that they did not need to translate the whole parent–teacher conversation but only the key topics and phrases that come up regularly, so they created sound files of the most common phrases in both languages and provide teachers and parents with a menu to find the file they need. This much simpler technological solution still addresses more than 80% of the real issues teachers are facing.

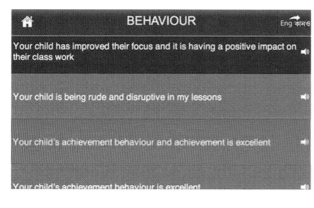

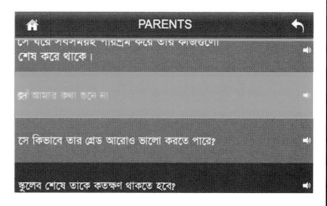

Make sure you can access data

Knowing where your data will come from before you begin building your app is critical, especially when the value of your app lies in its ability to process data. If you cannot access the data you need, then your app idea may be a non-starter.

These case studies show how important it is to think about data sources during the scoping process so that any problems are uncovered early and you can decide how to respond.

OysterCheck

The problem: The Oyster Card is an electronic 'ticket' that is used on public transport in London. You can pre-pay money onto your Oyster Card, but the ticket gates do not tell you when you are low on credit and Oyster Cards are regularly rejected because of insufficient credit. This is very irritating if you are in a hurry or there is nowhere to top up your card nearby. It is possible to check your balance online, but very few people do this. They would prefer to view their balance while they are on the move.

The solution: A mobile app that allows people with Oyster Cards to manage their account while they are out and about. Unfortunately, the solution relied on getting access to Oyster travel data, which is owned solely and exclusively by Transport for London. It is not public data. Without access to the data it was impossible to build OysterCheck.

StudioPhly

The problem: It is time consuming for young musicians to find and contact local recording studios that they can use.

The solution: A mobile app that allows young musicians to find and contact recording studios, but where was the data to come from? The StudioPhly team had two choices. They could rely on people already using the recording studios to generate the data or they could commit to creating the content themselves. The first option is preferable because it cuts down on the work StudioPhly have to do to get the app up and running and it ensures that the app will continue long after the initial batch of data they uploaded has dated. However, it means that the app has to be built with two different audiences in mind – the users of the content and the creators of the content – and the creators will be the more important of the two, at least initially.

▲ Pitching StudioPhly

Minimal Viable Product (MVP)

'Minimal Viable Product' or 'MVP' is a phrase that is used a lot in technology start-up companies. The Minimal Viable Product is the minimum technological solution you can provide and still demonstrate to your users that you are addressing their needs. An MVP can be launched faster and users can provide valuable feedback, which can be used to further develop the app.

Compute-IT

9.3.9 Does the solution need data to work? If yes:

a) Identify the data input, the data output and what happens to the data input to deliver the required data output.

b) Where will the data come from? Follow the decision tree to work out whether you have access to the data you need.

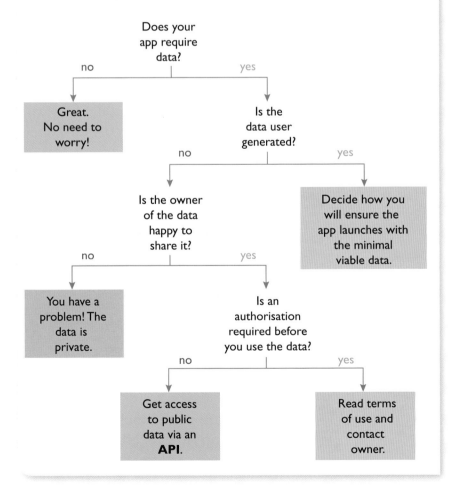

Key term

API (Application Programming Interface): Defines how software components can be programmed to interact with each other. A web API is a set of programming instructions and standards linked to a web-based software application. Software developers use a web API to design and build an app that is based on the original web-based software application. A searchable directory of web APIs can be found at: **www.programmableweb.com**.

Compute-IT

9.3.10 What is your Minimal Viable Product?

9.3.11 Do you need to revise your elevator pitch as a result of any changes you made to your solution as you completed 9.3.8 Compute-IT, 9.3.9 Compute-IT and 9.3.10 Compute-IT? Or do you need to abandon this idea and move onto another idea?

9.4 Product development

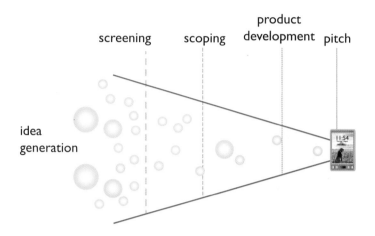

screening   scoping   product development   pitch

idea generation

User experience

You have worked hard to develop an app that is useful. Now it is time to make sure your app is both usable and desirable.

▲ iPads are very easy to use. Almost anyone, whatever their previous experience with computers, can pick up an iPad and use it without a book of instructions. The intuitive design means the iPad is very usable. They are also very desirable; they are a must-have piece of technology that people want to use and be seen using.

Screen maps and **wireframes** are useful tools to help you plan how the features of your app flow together and to ensure they deliver a positive user experience.

This case study shows how one company, Zolmo, set about creating an award-winning app.

Key terms

Screen map: Shows the flow of an app and how all the features are connected. Mapping the flow of your app ensures you don't miss an essential part of the app or add unnecessary features.

Wireframe: A visual guide showing how the features of a piece of software function and how the different aspects of a design link together.

Case study: Zolmo

In 2010, Zolmo won an Apple Design Award for the 20-minute meals app they created for Jamie Oliver.

Zolmo identified four features for the app:

- Browse recipes
- Create a shopping list
- Read a list of essentials you should have in your cupboard
- Browse cooking videos.

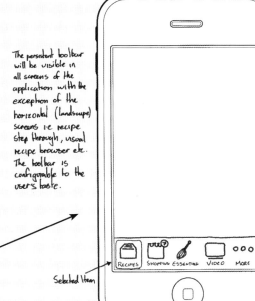

The persistent toolbar will be visible in all screens of the application with the exception of the horizontal (landscape) screens i.e recipe step through, visual recipe browser etc. The toolbar is configurable to the user's taste.

Selected Item

1. RECIPES Takes user to the recipe browser

2. SHOPPING Takes users to their shopping list

3. ESSENTIALS Store cupboard essentials are accessed from here.

4. VIDEO Takes users to the video browser

5. MORE Brings users to all further top level menu items (settings, about, feedback).

Zolmo's screen map clearly shows that browsing the recipes and getting instructions on how to cook them is the app's core feature.

Zolmo's wireframe then walks you through each screen. It includes each function and shows how the user interacts with it. While developing their wireframes, Zolmo will have challenged themselves to justify the inclusion of each function. If a function is not needed by the user or gets in the way of a positive user experience, it has to go.

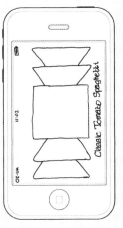

Setting and prioritising your objectives

It is nearly time to create your app, but first you need to set your objectives. It will be impossible to do everything you want to do straight away, so setting clear objectives enables you to prioritise what to focus on with each iteration of your app. You will also be able to evaluate each iteration against the criteria you set for yourself, to judge the quality of your app and to help you to set and prioritise your objectives for the next iteration.

When you set your objectives you will need to balance cost, time and quality. The perfect product is produced on time, within budget and to the required standard. But most products are not perfect. Often developers have to compromise. Deciding whether to compromise on cost, time or quality will depend entirely on the project

- Compromise on cost – spend more money to get the product out on time or up to the required standard.
- Compromise on time – deliver the product to the market later than planned but know it will be produced within budget and will be good quality.
- Compromise on quality – produce a less than perfect product but meet the budget and make sure users have it when they want it.

cost

time   quality

Challenge

It's finally time to create your app.

Plan-IT

9.4.1 Set and prioritise your objectives.

Plan-IT

9.4.2 Create a screen map and a wireframe for your app. Remember to think carefully about what your users want to do again and again and make it really easy for them to achieve this with the minimum number of interactions possible.

Compute-IT

9.4.3 Program your app using the tool or programming language of your choice.

Compute-IT

9.4.4 Test the first iteration of your app with your market. Evaluate the feedback you receive. Does your app meet your objectives? Then refine your solution, remembering to review your objectives with each new iteration.

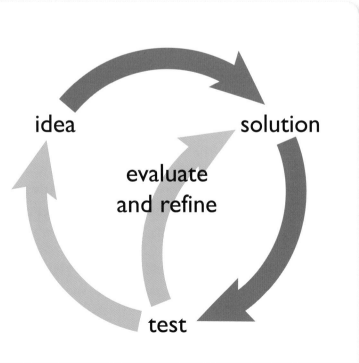

Glossary / Index

Acknowledgments

The Publishers would like to thank the following for permission to reproduce copyright material.

Photo credits:

All robot images used in Challenge boxes © julien tromeur – Fotolia.com.

p.4 *l* © Photo12/Elk-Opid/Alamy, *r* © REX/Associated Newspapers; **p.5** © Microstockeurope/ Alamy; **p.8** *t* © Tim Graham/Alamy, *m* © Interfoto/History/Alamy, *b* © Science Photo Library; **p.9** *t* © Cipher Wheel © Thomas Jefferson Foundation At Monticello, Made By Ronald Kirby, *b* © Chris Howes/Wild Places Photography/Alamy; **p.16** © Cipher Wheel © Thomas Jefferson Foundation At Monticello, Made By Ronald Kirby; **p.23** © fotandy – Fotolia.com; **p.33** © pizuttipics – Fotolia; **p.35** © Illustrated London News; **p.37** *t* © Arthur Reynolds Collection/ Lebrecht Music & Arts, *b* © Lebrecht Music & Arts; **p.38** *t* © Arthur Reynolds Collection/ Lebrecht Music & Arts, *b* © Lebrecht Music & Arts; **p.39** *t* © T.P/Lebrecht Music & Arts, *b* © Michael Nicholson/Corbis; **p.40** *t* © Arthur Reynolds/Lebrecht Music & Arts, *b* © Lebrecht Music and Arts Photo Library/Alamy; **p.41** © T.P/Lebrecht Music & Arts; **p.42** *t* © Pictorial Press Ltd/Alamy, *b* © Peter Holmes/Age fotostock Spain, S.L./Alamy; **p.43** © Illustrated London News; **p.44** *t* © Arthur Reynolds/Lebrecht Music & Arts, *b* © Edward Gooch/Getty Images; **p.49** *all image credits as given for pages 37 to 44*; **p.54** © philip kinsey – Fotolia; **p.72** © Sergey Dashkevich – Fotolia; **p.88** © KeystoneUSA-ZUMA/ REX; **p.100** *t* © Shangara Singh/Alamy, *b* © www.decdun.me.uk; **p.104** © David Stock/Alamy; **p.105** © David J. Green - electrical/Alamy; **p.107** © Graham Hastings; **p.110** *t* © Derek R. Audette/Fotolia, *b* © Adomanski/Fotolia; **p.111** © Graham Hastings; **p.114** © decade3d – Fotolia.com; **p.121** © Cynthia Johnson/Getty Images; **p.122** © Nick Higham/Alamy; **p.126** © Steven May/Alamy; **p.127** © PhotoQuest/Getty Images; **p.134** © Brocreative – Fotolia.com; **p.135** © Apps for Good; **p.136** © Jeremy Graham/Dbimages/Alamy; **p.144** © Apps for Good; **p.146** © Jackfrog/Fotolia; **p.147** © 2009 Jamie Oliver Limited.

Screenshot credits:

p.80 © Facebook www.facebook.com; **p.81** © Google www.google.com **p.129** *t* © Rovio Entertainment Ltd, *b* © Rumpus.

t = top, b = bottom, l = left, r = right, m = middle

Every effort has been made to trace all copyright holders, but if any have been inadvertently overlooked the Publishers will be pleased to make the necessary arrangements at the first opportunity.